WILL YOUNG
Anything Is Possible

with Marie-Claire Giddings

CONTENDER
BOOKS

First published 2002 by Contender Books
Contender Books is a division of
The Contender Entertainment Group
48 Margaret Street
London W1W 8SE

This edition published 2002
1 3 5 7 9 10 8 6 4 2

ISBN 1 84357 030 0

Printed in the UK by Butler & Tanner Ltd, Frome and London
Cover and plate section designed by Button Design
Typeset by seagulls
Edited by Wendy Hollas

Dedicated to Karen and Bobby.

Karen, a lady with the biggest heart, buckets of patience and who was always willing to listen and advise. A woman who will remain ingrained with me forever for her courage (mixed with stubborness?!), temperament and amazing sense of reality.

Bobby – my grandfather and a man who I loved and respected from day one (even when he made me eat my brussel sprouts and broccoli!). He will never leave my memory or my heart. I will love him to the day I die.

Love Will x

For Jessica and Jason and my wonderful family and friends. Without your incredible love and support (and exquisite coffee making) I wouldn't have been able to do any of this. Thank you all!

Love Marie-Claire x

INTRODUCTION

Last June, the morning after my final exams (I actually hadn't been to bed!), I found myself outside Exeter Cathedral. I remember it so clearly – it was 6am and I was sitting there looking at this fantastic building, eating a bacon sandwich, just thinking, I'm so happy. I had so much to look forward to and had already achieved so much. My third year at Exeter Uni had gone really well – I'd organised a charity ball (and raised £20,000 for Positive Action Southwest, an AIDS and HIV charity that the university raises money for every year), played the lead role in *Oklahoma!* and finished my degree course in politics. It had been a lot to take on – and if I'd stopped to think about it I probably wouldn't have done it – but rising to each challenge had paid off and I felt happier about myself than I had in a long time. I'd come a long way, considering I'd suffered a bit of a confidence crisis the year before, but I felt positive and excited about my future, particularly as I had a place at drama college. But nothing could have prepared me for what was about to happen and the choices I was about to make. Looking at my life now, it seems bizarre that I hadn't even heard of *Pop Idol* back then.

I think in the back of my mind I've always wanted to be an entertainer –although I did toy with the idea of being a vet for a while until I decided I wasn't clever enough! It wasn't necessarily fame I was interested in – it was being able to appear in front of an audience. My first performance was at Kingsbury Hill School as a fir tree in *Rumpelstiltskin*. I was only four but I still remember my green velvet outfit and my one line: 'As time went by the beautiful princess grew into a lovely girl.' Ah, my first step into theatre! My first step into the world of music, I suppose, was singing in the choir at Horris Hill prep school, and in the last years there I sang in various productions. People ask me if I've always had a good voice but I honestly don't remember. I suppose I was told I had a talent at prep school, but I was always a bit embarrassed about it – I don't know why! I was very shy, which might have had something to do with it (I think it's a bit of a family trait, to be honest) and it wasn't until I became a teenager that I began to blossom. For example, when I was younger I'd never even considered that I could be good at sport but I really got into it when I was about eleven, and even became captain of the school basketball and athletics teams later on. I really thrived as I grew older. I remember when I was seventeen having to give speeches once a week in assembly (something I could never have done when I was younger) and I got such a buzz when people laughed at my jokes. That was when I began to realise just how much I enjoyed performing.

Not that I did that much about it, mind you. I've only been to four auditions so I know I'm incredibly lucky to have won *Pop Idol*. I suppose the best-known competition I went in for (apart from the *Pop Idol* one, of course!) was for a boy band on *This Morning* back in 1999. I heard Richard and Judy announce it on their show when I was too hungover to go to lectures (most unlike me!), so I sent off a tape of me singing and got through to the last 75, which was a bit of a shock. I went up to London for my first ever audition, and then they whittled it down to nine of us for the TV show. We took part in a mini audition live on *This Morning* and I got through to the final four – with Lee Ryan, now the lead singer in Blue! Who would have thought that audition would come back to haunt me now? But I enjoyed every minute of it (apart from the hairstyle they gave me!) and it made me think more seriously about pursuing a career in music.

It did mean that my studies suffered, though. At university Dr Larvi Sadiki, my Middle East politics lecturer, said to me, 'If that's [singing] what you want to do then that's great,' but I know he thought I could have done well in politics. But it was a choice between music and studying to get a 2:1 and in the end music distracted me too much. Still, I ended up with a high 2:2, which isn't so bad. I'd decided to study politics because I thought I should know about what was going on in my country – and I'm glad I did it because it has already affected a lot of my views and opinions. One of my politics lecturers, Rhonda, was really supportive of my interest in music – she even wrote me a reference when I went to the Guild Hall to audition as a jazz singer. Unfortunately, I missed the audition because I turned up on the wrong day! All the way from Devon to London and back again the same evening and I didn't even get the chance to show what I could do because of my own stupidity. As you'll see in this diary, I'm a bit dizzy – but I made sure I had the date of the first *Pop Idol* audition imprinted on my brain!

What you're about to read (and I really do hope you enjoy it!) is my diary of an amazing few months that I will honestly never forget. I still can't quite believe (and I find it quite scary, if I'm honest) that people would want to read about me, Will Young, but I hope you find it an interesting insight into the whole *Pop Idol* experience. This is an honest account of what happened – and hopefully there'll be a few surprises and revelations along the way. I'm not sure what you already know about me (and probably a lot of what you've read isn't true!) and I don't know what you'll make of me once you've read it, but personally I think I'm quite modest, a real thinker, very sensitive and quite humorous. However, you might disagree! I don't like to take life too seriously otherwise it gets a bit boring, don't you think? I'm very passionate and very stubborn, as you'll find out. I also appreciate my religion – it's very important and extremely personal to me so I don't want to bang on about it, but I do think that it helped me throughout the competition. Actually, the whole contest was a very spiritual experience on any level – not necessarily a religious one. I found myself wondering: Why do I sing? Who gave me this voice? Why should I get all these perks for singing? It really did make me question things and consider that maybe you do have a kind of purpose – and mine can't be to just sing and make a lot of money for myself. Maybe I can try to use my new found fame to change things and help people. If you can move people in any way then that's a really special thing. Even if you only move one person, it's a real gift and you should always treasure it and use it accordingly, not abuse it.

What else can I tell you about myself? I think I've always been quite old for my age – a bit of a thinker! And I've always loved listening to music. These days I have such a varied taste in music, which is brilliant because I can now appreciate music on a much wider scale. At the moment I'm playing Groove Armada, David Gray, Mary J. Blige, Eurythmics, Erykah Badu, Jill Scott, John Lee Hooker, Leftfield, Sinatra, Terence Trent D'Arby, Vivaldi, Sheryl Crow – you can't get much more of a mixture, to be honest. My favourite record of all time has to be 'Love And Affection' by Joan Armatrading. What a song! As well as my love of music, I still love my own space to chill – I suppose I'm the same as everybody in that. It doesn't matter what walk of life you come from, you never have enough time to do exactly what you want to do all the time. I've always got drawings I want to work on, photographs I want to take, scripts I want to write, places I want to see. I think it's nice to have varied interests – unfortunately, though, I'm going to have even less spare time now that I'm a fully fledged pop star! Not that I'm knocking it – *Pop Idol* has changed my life in a way I could never have imagined. Certainly when I first entered the competition I never thought about how popular it might become – just as well because I probably would have bottled it if I'd known it was going to sweep the nation like it did. To me it was just another audition, except there were television cameras following us around everywhere. Thinking about it now, I'm not surprised it worked because it had everything – the good, the bad, the funny, the sad... It had continuity but it also changed every week, and best of all the public got to vote for their favourite so it became a talking point all over the country. I think it was edited fantastically well and I don't think people realise just how powerful editing can be. I was more than happy with the way I was portrayed – and I think the fact that I wasn't shown in the beginning worked in my favour because when I did finally appear I had my own things to say.

Anyway, enough of me for the moment...There are so many people in this diary who helped me through this incredible rollercoaster of a year and kept my feet on the ground. In my final year at uni I shared a house with Pilky (Claire) and Milsy (Camilla) who have remained great friends, along with my other uni mates Katy, Cally, Adam, Hugh, Andy D, Scottish Tom, Di and Fi. Mary and Andy M have both managed to put up with me since school and James is my oldest friend in the world. All at Arts Ed and then there's Mum and Dad, who still can't quite believe what's happened! I was lucky because I always had my twin brother Rupert to muck about with, and he has been constantly there by my side (or in the audience!) throughout the whole *Pop Idol* experience. We never had any jealousy between us and we still haven't now – Rupert's pleased for me but doesn't for a minute wish he was the pop star. Yes, we were both born on 20 January 1979, but we've always been individuals in our own right and will both go our own separate ways in life. Then there's my wonderful grand-mother, Meme, who has helped me in so many ways and is one of the loves of my life. How she put up with the terrible twins is beyond me! My sister Emma and her boyfriend Chappell, my nephew Jack, my Aunt and Uncle Wiggy and Tim, my Uncles Dominic and Jeremy and the rest of my fantastic friends: Bunny, Fraaaaan, Fran P, Stav, Emily, Tom Squires, Hope, Chevie, Ose, Abi, Funky Ram Girl, Katie W, Gemma, Gerrard, Hestar Robinson (someone who taught me about life and how to live it – thank you), Mrs Young, Laura B, Aunt Elle, Sara T and Janie (No.1 fan).

Just think… this is only the start!

WEDNESDAY, 20 JUNE 2001

Emily told me about a 'Pop Idol' competition today – she'd seen it in an advert in the *News of the World* and thought it would be right up my street. Apparently it's a big talent search to find a pop idol – like *Popstars*, I think. I just rang the number that was in the paper – well, I didn't have anything to lose by calling, did I? The first thing I did was laugh. There was DJ Neil Fox on the end of the phone saying, 'Hi, this is Foxy,' and immediately I thought, Oh my God, what kind of competition is this? But I took down the details and decided to check out the website for an application form. I printed it out and I couldn't believe there were so many questions to fill in! Maybe I'll leave it till the morning…

THURSDAY, 28 JUNE 2001

In the words of Michael Caine – 'I've only gone and bloody done it!' It took a while but I have finally filled in the application form – don't ask me how but I did. I really did have to think about the answers. I've just done my finals but even they didn't seem to take as long as it did to fill in this application form. I mean, I've never had to think about who my pop idol is – there are so many but I put down Tina Turner in the end for her strengths and ambitions. So I've sent it off – it's the deadline at the end of the week. Hope it gets there in time! I missed out on *Popstars* (well, I suppose it sort of passed me by if I'm honest!) and I auditioned for that boy band on *This Morning* and nothing came of that – I wonder if this'll go anywhere. I hope so. What an incredible opportunity. I spoke to Adam and Katie today and told them I had a really good feeling about this competition. I mean, it's such a perfect thing for me.

Oh well, it's in the post now. Fingers crossed x

TUESDAY, 31 JULY 2001

I still haven't heard anything from that Pop Idol thing – maybe they didn't like the sound of me? I've graduated now (that was a messy day and night – let's just say that me and vodka are no longer good friends!). Now that I've left uni it's very strange not having all my friends around me and handing in essays. I've got this great job in a restaurant called Harry's but I really must make a conscious effort to sort stuff out for drama school – I can't wait tables, make bad cocktails and muck up starters for ever! Still, at least I know how to make a decent cappuccino! I can't believe I start at Arts Ed in September. Must remember to get going on my sponsorship letters otherwise I'm not going to have any money to get me through, am I? I'm only halfway through the phone book and the ones I've spoken to so far don't seem that keen. Oh God, I must ask Mary if we're still on to share her flat in west London – hope she hasn't forgotten!

TUESDAY, 7 AUGUST 2001

Oh my God, it came! I got a letter this morning and it was a complete surprise when I opened it – I've been accepted for an audition for this Pop Idol competition! Hang on! Let me get the letter because I need to write this date in. I can't afford to forget it – not after what happened at the Guild Hall for that jazz-singing job!! Getting the day wrong is not a good way to be going about getting any career, let alone a music career. Anyway, the letter says I've been accepted for an audition and could I come to London on September 5? I've got just under a month to go and what the hell, I'm going to go for it, for the experience if nothing else. You never know – it might give me the confidence to try elsewhere if it comes to nothing.

SATURDAY, 1 SEPTEMBER 2001

I did definitely write down the fifth, didn't I?

TUESDAY, 4 SEPTEMBER 2001

It's tomorrow! I'm going to sing Aretha Franklin's 'Until You Come Back To Me' because it's one of my all-time favourites. I mustn't forget that I need to take my passport – only for identification unfortunately, not to be whisked away to pastures new!

WEDNESDAY, 5 SEPTEMBER 2001

Arrrrggggghhhhhh!! Today was the day – I trawled all the way up to the ExCeL Conference Centre in Docklands on the Light Railway, passport in hand. I was there all day. I registered and was given a number – I am now officially known as number 6691. As The Prisoner once said, 'I am not a number, I am a free man!' Oh my God, there were so many people – I really did wonder if we would all get seen. I spent most of the time by myself just people-watching – there were some pretty outrageous costumes around. Bikinis and not much else, shiny boy-band suits, crazy bright pink outfits – not nice! Eventually the dreaded moment came and a group of us were called to the first audition (apparently this is the last selection auditions for London so I was lucky to be there). Off we went up in the lifts to these two rooms where we were separated into either one. Apparently, these auditions would decide whether we go through to the next room in front of a producer, who will then decide if we're good enough to go in front of a panel of judges! I walked into my designated room and met the assistant producer Claire Howell – what a petrifying lady, not in the way she looked but because she was so cold and clinical about the whole situation. But then why shouldn't she be? She can't show any favouritism to anyone at this early stage. I sang 'Until You Come Back To Me'. I practised as much as possible all day, which gave me something to do while I waited around. I was one of the last to be called (one of the advantages I've had all my life of both my names starting with letters towards the end of the alphabet!) and I have to tell you it didn't go well at the beginning. But just as I got to the rifty bit I think I managed to pull it back. Well, I definitely managed to pull it back because she gave me a green form, which meant I was through to the next audition. Hurrah! But Claire told me to dance a bit and be a bit livelier in my next performance. Even I can manage that! Then it was off to meet one of the researchers, Helen, and fill in more questionnaires – blimey, how much do they need to know about me? I can't believe it – I'm through to round two but I need to make sure that I get through to the one after that where we get to perform in front of the judges. Well, I'm not going to wonder about them now because I'm out celebrating tonight!

FRIDAY, 7 SEPTEMBER 2001

We had another two rounds today and I have to say I was really scared. I've never needed the loo so much! Same system, same number, same room, but today it was the producer who was seeing us. I was the last one in (as per usual!) and I needed something to get me noticed so I'd decided to wear my granddad's jumper! As I walked into the room the producer looked up, and do you know what his words to me were? 'You'd better make this a good one cos I've had some terrible people in here today.' Oh great, no pressure then! I changed my song today – why I don't know. I plumped for Jackson 5's 'Blame It On The Boogie' because a. it's a great pop song and b. I knew the words already!

Anyway, I sang about ten seconds of it, threw some terrible shapes and then the producer said, 'That's brilliant, fine.' Thank God for that! I honestly thought I'd blown it! Then it was off for more questionnaire filling (this is worse than applying for a job!) and an interview with Camilla the researcher. Then I was told I'd be going in to see the judges, which was great because that's what I'd promised myself all along – just to try and get to perform for the judges. The TV cameras were filming us all quite a lot, which made me feel nervous – especially as they were being thrust in our faces just as we were about to walk through the door and audition. I really wanted to concentrate on the singing, not being on a TV show. One by one we went in – guess who was last through! But just before I went in, someone called Simon (who I later found out was one of the directors on the show) asked me some quite silly questions like, 'Are you nervous?' Of course I bloody am! I'm not sitting here for the fun of it, you know! But as I walked through the door I have to tell you that nothing prepared me for what was going to be in that room.

My heart was beating louder than a big bass drum – was I really the only person that could hear it? It felt like I walked into the room in slow motion. I was instantly blinded by the brightest lights you've ever seen – even when I performed in *Oklahoma!* at uni the stage lights weren't that bright. There were cameras and people everywhere and then of course… THE JUDGES.

I knew who three of them were – Simon Cowell, a suntanned, record-company bigwig who I originally met on that competition on *This Morning* (he was one of the judges on that too – wonder if he recognised me? He hasn't changed much but he's slightly more orange than last time!), Nicki Chapman, a soft-looking blonde lady who I only knew of because she had been a judge on *Popstars*, and Neil Fox, who I recognised from *The Pepsi Chart Show*. A bespectacled grey-haired man (who I later found out to be record producer Pete Waterman) was the first to speak. 'William Robert Young, you have come before this court today and you are the last person we are going to see in this entire competition so it had better be a good one.' Oh great, NO PRESSURE AT ALL!!! And to make matters worse, everybody had piled into the room to watch because I was the very last audition – it felt like there were 100 people in the room but there were only about fifteen or twenty.

So I just smiled and took a big deep breath. I sang 'Blame It On The Boogie' and I have to say it went alright – Pete Waterman said the vocal was nice, Nicki Chapman said the same and so did Neil Fox. Then Pete brought up my clothes. 'A pair of old jeans, a pair of shoes that have never seen polish in their lives, a top that's seen better days and a shirt that's got egg stains on it. You think I'm gonna put you through? No way, kid!' I just thought, Oh hell! Then Nicki said, 'I didn't like your moves but you're going through.' I felt disappointed and elated all at the same time. Then Neil Fox called me cheesy – talk about kettle, pot, black!!! And then it was the turn of Simon Cowell, the chairman of the judges (so Claire Howell told me earlier), and judging by the looks on some faces today, he's not a particularly nice man! Anyway, he was really milking it by taking his time before saying anything. I just thought, Oh come on, you fool, get on with it! And then came, 'You're a good-looking lad, but do you want it?' Well, what did he want me to do? Beg for a place? I just kept smiling and said, 'Yes I do,' even though I didn't know exactly what it was I was supposed to want. Then Simon said, 'Good boy – I'll see you through. Take on the points we've said today.'

I did it – I bloody did it – even with Bobby's egg-stained top on! Was he watching from above? Now I've got to go back and do it all again on Monday! Told Cally (she has always been really supportive in my life) and she was so excited. She always says to me to just do it. Well, this time, Cally, I have! Don't think I'll say anything to Mum and Dad yet, though. I'm through to the final 100 but there are still another three rounds to go before they get it down to the final 50. As we were leaving I was told that I would have to perform The Drifters' 'Up On The Roof' and a song of my choice on Monday – now all I need to do is practise singing them!

MONDAY, 10 SEPTEMBER 2001

I really needed to practise before the audition today and I
found this great little chapel up the road from Mum and
Dad's which would be ideal (I must remember to take the
key back!). I must admit I told the curate a little fib and said
I was entering a classical competition – well, he was hardly
going to let me use it if I said I was practising to be a pop
star! I said a few prayers too, though, so it wasn't all bad!
It's such an amazing place – wonderful acoustics and
incredibly inspiring. I sang 'Up On the Roof' so many times
I thought I actually *was* on the roof! I also practised 'All Or
Nothing' – I'm not a massive fan of O-Town but this song is
a good one. I was really enjoying myself and could have
stayed all day, but suddenly realised (I always leave things
until the last minute, don't I?) I had to get a move on and get
to London if I didn't want to miss the audition!

I tried to take on board everything the judges had said on
Friday. Dance moves – tried a bit harder, clothes – no more
egg-stained shirts. I chose a bit of a sad outfit (I can say it

now I'm writing this), but this morning it's what I thought the judges would like me to wear – white trousers with black loafers and a grey jumper. Felt like a model out of an early 90s' Top Man window display, but I thought I should make an effort rather than turn up in my usual baggy trousers and tank tops.

I was also trying to move bits into my new home today. I'm very excited – it's the most beautiful flat in west London. Mary certainly knows a good buy, that's for sure. And she's already moved in so I need to get a move on especially as I start at Arts Ed next Monday. I can't believe I start college in a week's time – oh my God! Anyway, I packed everything up, along with a tape of the two songs I was going to be singing so I could practise all the way to Battersea where I usually leave my car if I'm going into central London. Got there and the road had been changed to residents' parking permits only. If you could have seen my face – I had an hour to get to the St Giles Hotel on Tottenham Court Road, which is where the *Pop Idol* people have put us up for three nights, and nowhere to park my car. I just thought, sod it, parked the car as normal and charged off. Got there 45 minutes late, checked in and then was told to get ready in the clothes I'd be wearing tomorrow. Went straight up to the room, threw my 'Top Man' outfit together and went back downstairs for a meeting. Well, if you could have seen all these beautiful people – perfectly made-up girls, cool-looking boys and me in possibly the nastiest clothes there – I just thought I'd made the biggest mistake of my life choosing that outfit. It was awful! They were all talking away to each other – I'm sure they were all looking at me. OK, maybe I'm being a bit paranoid!

We had a Q&A session with the judges – anything that we wanted to know we were allowed to ask. I sat right at the back and well out of the way of the cameras – they seem to be everywhere now. This girl asked a perfectly normal question – if whoever won the competition would be able to write their own songs or at least be able to contribute to them at some point. Pete Waterman suddenly went off on one at this girl about not being concerned with song writing, which I thought was a bit unfair because on the application form it was one of the questions they asked us. I was ready to lay into Pete and say as much! My hand was in the air but nobody picked me – THANK GOD! I was ready to let rip to try and defend this girl so it's probably a good thing they didn't choose me. Anyway, it all continued with everybody being slightly more wary about what they asked in case Pete went off on one again! The judges answered questions like, 'What are you looking for?' and 'Are we going to be dancing?' – it was very helpful to hear what they had to say.

After the Q&A session we had a meeting about what's happening tomorrow. Then we had to have our photographs taken – wonder what they're for? Got told that the first round was our own choice of song – that was going to be the O-Town one for me – and then the second round would be The Drifters song. We've got to get through that first round or we're out on our ears – what a thought. I didn't come this far to be left behind. Left the others reasonably early and here I am now – better go, got to get my beauty sleep! Judging from the competition I'm going to need it.

TUESDAY, 11 SEPTEMBER 2001

Arrived at the Criterion Theatre, where the auditions were being held, about 7.30 this morning. Didn't eat before I got there – was too nervous. Got put into a group of nine and we were the last lot on stage – funny, that! We had to sing the song we'd chosen. There were seven contestants before me. The immortal line 'Step forward 6691' came and I began 'All Or Nothing' by O-Town. Just as I was getting into the swing of things a big 'thank you' boomed through the theatre. Didn't know if they liked me or not because I didn't get anywhere with the song. Then, 'Thank you, everyone – please exit to the left.' It just had me wondering what the hell was going on – did they like us or not? We didn't get any feedback, which was very annoying.

When we came out we all went straight back upstairs and waited in the lower bar (which wasn't open unfortunately!). Sat by myself and kept out of the way of everybody else and drank water till it came out of my ears. Then they filed us all back in again, and yes, we were the last group, but we didn't know what was happening. All these rumours had been filtering through that if you were asked to stand forward then you were out or you were a might be. We didn't have a clue what was going on and waiting on stage was horrific. They got a girl called Nicola (whose best moment of the competition was 'You think I can't sing but you're wrong, mate') to step back and I thought, Well, maybe I've got through. But they made us go back and forward and I have honestly to say I just thought, You idiots. Then Simon Cowell told us that eight of us were through and you know what, I was absolutely ready for anything – bring it on!!!

So after lunch, which I couldn't eat cos I was too nervous (I'm sure this competition isn't good for my health!), the boys were split into groups of three to sing 'Up On The Roof' by The Drifters and the girls sang 'Say A Little Prayer' by Aretha Franklin. I was with this guy called Craig and, strangely enough, Andy Derbyshire, who I recognised from my audition for Arts Ed. He didn't remember me but I'm terrible like that – I will remember someone's face from five years ago and say to them, 'Remember me? I bumped into you down Oxford Street five years ago,' and they just look at me blankly! But I was worried that he was in my group because he was brilliant and glamorous and looking very cool and there I was in my minging white trousers, black loafers and nasty grey jumper. Arrggghhh, why did I choose that outfit? Anyway, minging outfit aside, we worked out a

'Graduation day – let's party!'

'Don't we all scrub up well at the Black Hawk Down premiere?' _ above
'Early photo of me on stage – how things have changed!' _ top left
'Me with the fantastic voice coaches, David and Carrie.' _ bottom left

'Warming up before the S Club 7 concert in Dublin.'

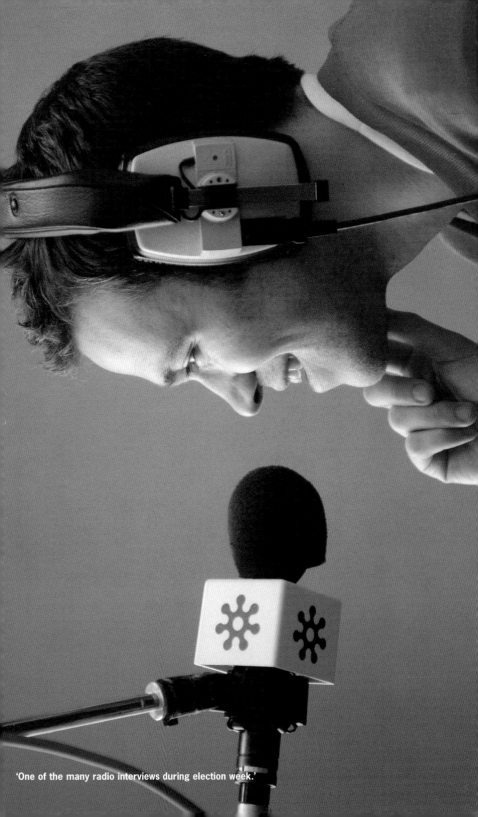

'One of the many radio interviews during election week.'

'Catching 40 winks on the battle bus.'
'Another day, another interview…' _ opposite

'The battle continues.'

little routine between us in the corridors, and when we went in, Andy started to sing first and then we took it in turns. I was really pleased with it, I have to say – much more me. Still no feedback, which was so frustrating, and then we came back offstage and were interviewed by Ant and Dec, who will be hosting the TV show! They seem like nice people. In fact, they're exactly how you see them on TV – funny, nice and extremely professional. I must find out when the first show is going to be on.

And then we went to the bar which is where I heard about the terrible thing that happened in America – it was all a bit too much to take in. There we were battling it out in this theatre in London, where the only care in the world was getting through to the next round, while two planes had flown into the twin towers of the World Trade Center. Everybody just sat around in disbelief. We had loads of time before we would hear anything so I went back to the hotel and switched on the TV straight away. I honestly thought that what I was watching was a film... I felt physically sick and the auditions suddenly seemed utterly trivial and meaningless. I decided I didn't want to be on my own and went to my soon-to-be new home and sat and watched the telly in shock with Mary. If I was going to be with someone it had to be one of my oldest friends from school.

Before I went back to the theatre, I decided to change my clothes – it sounds weird but I just thought I would be more relaxed in my every day slouchy clothes. So turned up wearing my orange tank top, jeans, trainers and my favourite bobble hat. The results were supposed to have been at 6.30pm, but do you know what, they kept us waiting for three hours! Three hours – what a bloody cheek. As if everything that had happened today wasn't traumatic enough. 9.30pm came, and Claire the producer came in and said, 'If we call out your name please go into these rooms.' The first group was called out and I was in it – there were twelve others with me. I have to say I didn't think this was a great sign, because they were trying to get it down to the final 50 so they had a lot of people to get rid of. To make matters worse they made us pack our bags so that if we didn't make it through they could film us leaving the competition. Nice! But guess who didn't pack his bag?

Oh and before I forget, I have to tell you who was in my group – Darius Danesh, the bloke from *Popstars*! If I'm honest I really did think that was a definite sign that we were all going – well, he hadn't done that well in *Popstars*, had he? We didn't talk though because as usual I kept myself to myself. It almost felt as though we had a celebrity in our group because of all the coverage he's had.

Then they must have been going round the rooms telling whoever was in they were in because there was this almighty cheer and we just thought, that's it. I was so angry because I just thought, bugger, I know what I'm capable of and I haven't done any of it. Then the camera crew came in, followed by the judges, who just took one bloke out – I have no idea what that was all about but it didn't help our nerves that they kept us waiting for another twenty minutes. I didn't know what to think and the cameras were still on us. Then Simon Cowell walked in. I have to tell you word for word what happened next. He says, 'I'm so sorry...' Biggest pause in the world. '...to keep you waiting all this time.' (get on with it Mr Cowell) 'We've been backwards and forwards and had to make some difficult decisions tonight, I'm afraid. However, you should be pleased to know that you are through to the next round.' I can't tell you how I felt. I just clutched my head in my hands and jumped around along with everybody else and hugged anyone that was near me. If that wasn't enough drama, Pete Waterman then had to add his tuppence worth! 'Hang on – you only scraped through so you're here because you just got the nod.'

Then Simon hits us with, 'It was really difficult making our minds up because certain people blew it and then we thought they were great and vice versa. So every one of you has got a chance but believe me, you're going to have to work that much harder than everyone else. Congratulations!'

I hate to say it but I just burst into tears – what am I like? Then I walked out and was in a bit of daze. It was all too much for me to take in but I thought, Bloody hell, I'd better pull my finger out. Why put us through if we were in the 'maybe' room? They didn't have to but they did and it completely geared me up to work much harder. If that was their plan it worked with me. So we're down to the final

61 and that means that tomorrow eleven of us will be leaving and to top it all Darius proved me wrong – how guilty did I feel?

The boys were given three songs to choose from for tomorrow – 'Rock DJ' by Robbie Williams, 'Fast Love' by George Michael and 'Sex Bomb' by Tom Jones. I've plumped for 'Fast Love' because I've listened to it so many times and I already know the words – always helpful – plus the other two songs aren't particularly suited to my voice. Decided to have a little run-through but it's late now (about midnight) and I need to sleep. Today was completely draining – physically and mentally – and right now I need my bed. Night.

WEDNESDAY, 12 SEPTEMBER 2001

Didn't sleep well in the night and just had 'Fast Love' flowing round my head – arrrgggghhh, how annoying! Didn't have breakfast – I was far too nervous – and arrived at the Criterion about 8.30am.

There were some really nice people in the George Michael group – a couple of guys called Korben and Aaron and a young guy called Oliver who has the most amazing voice. Craig (from my 'Up On The Roof' group) was there so it was nice to see a familiar face. There was also Darius and two others, Chris and Neil. Oh and I nearly forgot – I met Ant and Dec again, too. They're fantastic blokes. Dec cracked a joke about how he thought the George Michael group would be practising in the toilets – very amusing! Neil had a terrible time with his words and kept forgetting them, but that was part of the challenge and it seemed that nerves definitely got the better of him. We had to wait our turn in the corridor and I could hear the others singing. They all sounded great but for some reason it didn't bother me and I felt really confident. When I walked in, there they were, the judges, sitting about ten rows from the stage. And, believe it or not, today was the first time I had ever sung with a microphone, which was weird, but it sounded great – well, it sounded great from where I was! Sang my heart out and before I had a chance to worry about what it sounded like, I got that booming 'thank you' again (which really riled me!) so I left the stage and then we all had to wait about an hour before we found out if we were in or out. All 61 of us then went back on to the stage and were met by the judges. Neil Fox spoke first: 'For eleven of you on that stage it's going to be an awful day, for 50 of you it's going to be the most fantastic day. And I firmly believe that I will be playing probably more than one of you as a Number-One artist in the future because there is some real talent here, so thank you from me and good luck. Now we can sit back and see how the great British public love you or hate you.' I just thought, Oh my God, eleven of us have got to leave, and then Nicki Chapman spoke: 'I do have my pop idol in front of us which is a very pleasing thought. You should be very proud of yourselves and we obviously have to get it down to 50. But my idol is in this room so from a personal point of view I'm extremely happy for anyone that we're taking through.'

Then it was Pete: 'For those of you that don't get through please don't give up – keep trying. And to the rest of you and the winner I'm just proud at one point I can say I've had part of her career as well... or his.' Ah, what a lovely man, but then his royal ogreness speaks: 'So give yourselves a big round of applause.' That wasn't too bad, but then we had to go upstairs and wait for that dreadful decision. The smoking has started again – I've only lasted since July and I am absolutely going to blame this competition for me getting back into the habit!!!

Then, number by number, we were called back into the auditorium. I was with Layla, Joanne, Rosie, Chris, Tania, David, Vanessa, Sandi and Nicole and they told us we had made it to the next round. Simon Cowell's words were, 'As with any competition there are winners and there are losers. Someone has to go out. You are all winners, congratulations!' I was so happy – I was looking around for someone to hug and I didn't know any of them. Then we all went and sat in the auditorium because two more groups had to be brought out on stage. They brought a group of eleven people out and they were the group that didn't make it – it was terrible. I was definitely relieved to be sitting in the auditorium, but watching those people being told they hadn't made it was heartbreaking – if that had been me would I have been so strong? We were all in the same boat – we all wanted to sing but not all of us had made it. Did the lucky bobble hat strike again?

THURSDAY, 13 SEPTEMBER 2001

Went to pick up my poor deserted car today, fully expecting it to have been towed away. And blow me – it was still there in a residents' parking bay in south London with not so much as a parking ticket on it. I'm sorry but someone somewhere is looking after me, don't you think? And I had to tell someone that I had actually made it into the final 50 people in this competition – how fantastic is that? I am soooo happy – this is one of the biggest steps in my life. Drove over to Katie's house and I tried to explain the whole *Pop Idol* experience to her but I couldn't – I'm actually glad this is a TV show now because people can get a taste of just what we've been through. Found out that the first show will be shown on 6 October – wonder if I'll be on it and how I'm going to come across because I never really gave the TV cameras a second thought. Oh well, not a lot I can do about it now! Katie was really pleased for me though – it's great to have fantastic friends who support you in everything you do. I drove over to see Cally, too, and told her everything and she was jumping up and down saying, 'I told you you could do it!' and she was, as always, right! Decided to drive back home to see Mum and Dad. I told them exactly what I had been up to for the last week or so and I think they were surprised because of course they had no idea. Explaining the process to them was hilarious – they really didn't have a clue what I was on about! I just can't wait until they can watch the show and see how mental all this really is.

SATURDAY, 15 SEPTEMBER 2001

Moved into Mary's flat – didn't realise I had so much stuff. There are so many steps to climb that I'm absolutely shattered from all the exercise. It really is a beautiful place to live and Mary has decorated it in a very individual, arty and stylish way... and the views of London are breathtaking. Got settled in and then managed to go out for a pint down the road – a very important part of moving into a new house, I think!

MONDAY, 17 SEPTEMBER 2001

Started at Arts Ed in Chiswick today – scary! I didn't tell anyone that I was in the *Pop Idol* contest though because I wasn't sure how it would go down, plus I don't think you're supposed to go to any auditions whilst you're at drama college – so me and Andy (who's also in the final 50) have got to keep it quiet together. I suppose if either of us get any further we'll have to say something, though.

Anyway, today there were about 50 of us beginning college. We were all taken to this room and one by one we had to stand up and introduce ourselves to the rest of the people there. Then we were shown around the school – always helpful to know where you've got to be for lessons! I'm studying musical theatre, so all the dancing, singing and acting is going to take my mind off this competition. At least I've got something to go back to if it all ends tomorrow, and studying at college is going to be a great way to get a career somewhere in show business. After lunch we had a movement class, which was quite scary, and then the afternoon was spent being separated into groups which would become our classes. Then we had another movement and dance class, which I sweated all the way through because I'm so unfit (very embarrassing!). Then we had to introduce ourselves to the whole school – extremely daunting!

FRIDAY, 21 SEPTEMBER 2001

Sorry I haven't written – been so busy at college I haven't had time to pick up a pen and paper! I really am having such a great time. In fact, I can't believe that this time last week I was singing on stage at the Criterion Theatre – how funny. I have been told by the *Pop Idol* team that the heats for the final 50 will be starting soon so I guess I should be getting ready for that – or maybe, as usual, I'll leave it until the last minute!

Have had a brilliant time in this last week though – really like all of my class. Catrin and Lou are lovely and Fudge is a nice bloke. In fact, the whole class seem a really nice bunch of people. Met a wonderful girl in the second year called Marianne – she's lovely and she's been looking after me.

WEDNESDAY, 3 OCTOBER 2001

Oh my God, I've been told today that my group (which is group four of the five groups we have been split into) from the final 50 will start rehearsing on Monday 19 November! We'll have rehearsals on the Monday and Tuesday then it's going to be filmed on the Wednesday and then we have to wait until the Saturday for the voting – talk about keeping you on tenterhooks! Wonder what I'll have to sing? Oh well, at least I can get myself psyched up for it – all I have to deal with now is telling college. I really hope they don't kick me out. I'm going to have to take four days off and to lose four days of training is really quite sacred.

SATURDAY, 6 OCTOBER 2001

Can't believe the first *Pop Idol* show was on TV tonight – and guess what? I bloody missed it! Typical! I just completely forgot it was on, to be honest. But then I had loads of messages on my mobile from friends telling me that I wasn't even in it! I called some of them back and explained that the auditions were held all around the country and that the first few shows were of the regional auditions but I'm sure they think I've been making the whole thing up.

SUNDAY, 7 OCTOBER 2001

Remembered that the show was on (well done, Will!) and settled down to watch it with friends. The show was very funny – Ant and Dec are hilarious anyway but to watch them do this is very amusing. And some of the people they showed spent the next two months entertaining the nation they were so bad! Oh God, that sounds awful now I've written it! I guess I had the bottle to just go for it so why shouldn't anybody else? But still haven't been featured on the programme so far!

SATURDAY, 13 OCTOBER 2001

Third programme and I *STILL* haven't been on the show –
today I honestly thought that I was one of those mad people
who believe their own fantasies. Did I really take part in this
competition? You're bloody right I did and I've got the
confirmation letters to prove I got through, thanks very
much. I really have done a good job of keeping out of the
way of the cameras – mmm, maybe I was a bit too good at it!

SATURDAY, 20 OCTOBER 2001

I am slightly pickled. Have just got myself into a right old state watching the show where I found out that I had only just got through. I have just completely relived the emotions that I went through that very day and my body has now paid for it with six bottles of beer and a packet of fags – crikey, it was only an hour-long show! Why did I get so worked up? It's not as though I didn't know the outcome but I felt every nerve, every good bit, bad bit. It's like if you heard a certain bit of music and it suddenly reminded you of a particular point in your life. I was on my own cos Mary wasn't back from work so I had to watch it by myself. I was so nervous about how I was going to be portrayed – the power of editing is very strong indeed – but so far I haven't come across that badly at all. But I must say it's strange watching yourself on a TV programme – very peculiar!

THURSDAY, 1 NOVEMBER 2001

Am finding drama college very tough – they're such long days and I take my hat off to everyone there. It's very expensive too. Aged 22 and I am already £21,000 in debt – £11,000 to get through university and another £10,000 for my first year of Arts Ed. All for a bloody singing career! I'm getting up at 6.30/7am (a miracle for me seeing as I'm not very good at getting out of bed), getting everything I need for each particular day (guaranteeing that I will leave at least one thing behind!), and am out of the door by 7.30/7.45 and at the tube station before 8am. We have to be at college between 8.20 and 8.45: if we're late we get barred for the day and if that happens three times or more you're out of college altogether! I normally cut it very fine and arrive at 8.45. The day usually consists of a jazz or dance class until 10.30 and then maybe a tap class after that, followed by an acting class and then it's lunch. I'm enjoying the fact that we have so much physical stuff to do – I'm getting fitter with all this dancing, that's for sure! After lunch we have either a vocal session like voice work or speech work – something in a classroom, anyway – and then we end the day with a ballet or a contemporary dance class or a history of music and dance lesson and then it's all over about sixish.

I'm not getting back until 7.30pm, and although I'm loving it, the reality is I don't know how much longer I can stay at college and take part in this competition.

SATURDAY, 3 NOVEMBER 2001

Missed the show (no surprise there!) but have found out who the first two to go through are. Gareth Gates (the guy with the stammer) is already the bookies' favourite to win – what an incredible pressure for him to deal with. As if he hasn't got enough to worry about. But he does look like he's got the whole package – the voice, the looks and the love of the public already! He sang 'Flying Without Wings' – a Westlife track. The other person through is Zoe Birkett – I can't believe she's only sixteen with a voice like that. Rupert watched the show and said her version of 'One Moment In Time' blew him away. I've watched them on some of the earlier shows and they are two incredible singers – whoever gets into this final ten is definitely going to have their work cut out if the standard is as high as this.

Have also been told today that I've got to choose three songs – well, actually I need to give the TV show a list of ten songs that I wouldn't mind singing and then they choose three from that. MUST DO THAT NOW!

MONDAY, 5 NOVEMBER 2001

Got given back my three songs and this is what they've chosen for me to sing out of a list of songs from Wham!, Seal, The Doors, George Michael, Elton John, India Arie and Joan Armatrading:

Wham!'s 'I'm Your Man' – a great song
The Doors' 'Light My Fire' – just the one I wanted
George Michael's 'Careless Whisper' – what a song!

I think I'm going to choose 'Light My Fire' – mind you, it's the most un-pop-like song out of the three. Wonder how that will go down?

SATURDAY, 10 NOVEMBER 2001

It's the second week of the final 50 and tonight I sat down and watched the show with Mary – I can't believe what the judges were saying to people but I suppose that's why they're there. Two very sexy ladies got through tonight – Laura Doherty, who sang a great song, 'Son Of A Preacher Man', and Hayley Evetts – wow, what a girl. Her voice is incredible and really suited her song, 'I Have Nothing' by Whitney Houston. She's the first person to make me stop watching the competition and actually listen to the voice!

FRIDAY, 16 NOVEMBER 2001

Been practising all day with Marianne from college – she's such an amazing person. She reckons I've got to do 'Light My Fire' – in fact, her exact words were, 'Be yourself, do it to the best of your ability and then the rest of it is completely out of your hands. Try and come across well on TV and just be honest.' I'm lucky that I've had five weeks at college (can't believe it's been five weeks already).

Preparation-wise it's really helped me in the competition – and all the singing and dancing practice is paying off.

SATURDAY, 17 NOVEMBER 2001

The two Welsh wonders went through tonight. Jessica Garlick sang 'Crazy For You' (she looks like a sweet girl and then she opens her mouth and hits you with a voice and a half!) and Rosie Ribbons sang a sensational version of the Bryan Adams' song 'Everything I Do'. It sent shivers up my spine! She's going to be a tough one to beat (listen to me like I'm already through and up against them!). Shame Andy from college didn't get through but he is such a star I think he'll be fine.

IT'S MY WEEK NEXT WEEK. I'm glad I've watched these last couple of shows because at least I've got a bit of an idea of what's going on. I know I've got to walk through the doors and on to the stage – easy! Watching the show tonight I still cannot believe how rude Simon Cowell is. I've discussed this with friends and family and they've said, 'You can't have a go at him, you can't.' But I was talking to my dad earlier and I said to him that I didn't think he had brought me up to let people speak like that to me and he agreed. So if that Cowell says one thing on the show I'm going to say something back! Have seen who else is going to be in my group (they showed it at the end of the show!) and the only two people I recognise are Craig and Korben. I'm excited and nervous but completely ready for it all at the same time. Come on, Will, sort yourself out, this could be your big chance!

SUNDAY, 18 NOVEMBER 2001

Got to the hotel this evening and met up with everyone in my group (the funny thing is it's a different group of people to the ones they showed on the programme last night) and they all seem like a nice bunch. Natalie Anderson, Sally Goodison, Callandria Jones, Rebecca Govan (who replaced poor Layla – she lied about her age and the TV show found out that she was only fifteen and chucked her out). Erm, who else? Tania Foster, Korben, Lucinda O'Connell, Scott Sadari and Craig Thomas. Sally seems like a laugh and Becky is very sweet, and it was great to see Craig and Scott again. Decided I should get an early night and have been in bed since 10pm, which is where I'm writing this. So no more pillow talk but more hot news tomorrow!

MONDAY, 19 NOVEMBER 2001

Oh my God, it's my week and there's so much to do! We left the hotel and arrived at the TV studios in Teddington where we had our run-throughs with David, Carrie and Mike, the musical team. David Grant was a successful singer back in the 80s, firstly with a group called Lynx and then as a solo artist. Later he joined forces with Carrie, his wife, to launch their group Suga Shak. They had one club hit and are now running their own gospel group! They're here to help us with our vocal ability, and they are so joyful and give out such amazing energy that you just can't help but listen to them. Mike transposes the music – so he works out which part of the song is best for us to sing in the one minute and twenty seconds we have to perform, and which key we should sing it in. I could tell just from this first meeting what an incredibly talented man he is and he completely put me at ease. He's a brilliant teacher and I felt so comfortable standing next to that piano because it's what I've been doing for the last couple of months every day at college. All three of them said they were so pleased that someone had chosen something so different to sing – which I took as a compliment from people who know their music inside out.

We all had a run-through and everybody sounded great. This is what we're all going to be singing:

Lucinda – 'How Do I Live', LeAnn Rimes

Sally – 'Sisters Are Doin' It', Aretha Franklin and Annie Lennox

Natalie – 'Hero', Mariah Carey

Korben – 'From The Heart', Another Level

Rebecca – 'Out Of Reach', Gabrielle

Craig – 'I Believe I Can Fly', R Kelly

Scott – 'You Got A Friend', James Taylor

Callandria – 'Think Twice', Celine Dion

Tania – 'Killing Me Softly', Dionne Warwick

We also had a chat about our styling for the show – I'm still not sure what I'm going to wear but I think I might go for something smart and casual. Not very me though but I do need to make a bit more of an effort – especially if they think the best I can do fashion wise is that dreadful outfit I wore at the Criterion! Still can't believe that I thought it looked good – white trousers, grey jumper and a pair of black loafers. My outfits will never look so bad again, I promise, especially now we have professional stylists!

We were taken around the studios – it amazes me how small these places actually are compared to how big they look on television! Then we were shown the Green Room, which is normally where guests on a TV show would chill out, but on this show it's where Ant and Dec will be interviewing us.

My sing-through of 'Light My Fire' went very well, and I think once we've gone through the dynamics it will be great. I want to take it very soft and jazzy at the beginning and then build up to the chorus – 'Time to set the night on (breathe) fire,' take it up the octave and then blast the chorus, 'The time to hesitate is through.' I want to really play on 'Try now you can only lose' because it's a really good phrase so I must use it. I must be careful not to get too gospel. I think I should tone it down a bit on the big chorus because it will make it more manageable (whatever rifts I do should be manageable on the ear). It's really nice to be working with people who are so passionate about music and hear where you're coming from – and you can understand where they're coming from. Already this has been brilliant, and I feel confident that I'll do myself justice.

Nicki Chapman and Olivia from 19 came around today and we had a chat. I couldn't keep my mouth shut and had to ask her about Simon Cowell and why he's so blunt with everybody. And actually it was useful because she said that's just what he's like and it made it a bit more understandable.

Now back at the hotel and just had a chat with Charlotte, the press lady – I decided to talk to her about me being gay. She had asked everyone before if there was anything they were worried about and while I'm not worried about it, I am quite private and want to know how to deal with this. She was really cool and we talked about everything – including how best to keep my private life private at this stage of the competition – she completely reassured me though. It's one thing telling your friends and family that you're gay but it's slightly daunting imagining it written in the press when I've never been in a national newspaper in my life.

TUESDAY, 20 NOVEMBER 2001

Pretty much the same again today as yesterday – singing and perfecting the song with David, Carrie and Mike. Decided on my outfit (black shirt and the flared black trousers Mum bought for me) and we had a dress rehearsal. We're recording the show tomorrow so I need to get everything right. Am glad that I started this diary because I want to remember everything about this incredible experience – it'll definitely be something to tell the grandkids – well, maybe not mine! We had three run-throughs today – no judges, just cameras! I practised 'Light My Fire' and Alan the floor manager was só helpful, telling me what I needed to do and where I needed to look. In fact, the whole team's fantastic – it feels like they really, really want us to do our best.

But a great day was tarnished by some very sad news – a very close family friend, Karen, had passed away. She was my father's secretary and my second mum. If I had phoned her and said, 'I've lost my head' she'd have said in her wonderful Scottish accent, 'OK, Will, don't panic. Stay where you are and I'll find it for you.' Such a wonderful lady cruelly taken away from us by a brain tumour – she didn't deserve to go.

I felt very down but the voice warm-up with Mike cheered me up because he made it so much fun. I have to say, I really notice the difference having been at college – I know I said it had prepared me better for this competition but I do feel confident. Just had interviews with Sally, the lady from the *Pop Idol* internet site, and with Kate Thornton for ITV2, which both went really well. It was strange being interviewed by Kate because she was also one of the judges on that *This Morning* competition – she doesn't remember me though! I cracked a few of my usual gags (too crap to mention obviously because I'm the only one who laughs at them!) but basically was just my usual stupid self.

I'm feeling really relaxed and I just want to *enjoy* performing my song tomorrow. It's a great song, I sing it well and I never get to sing with a microphone, especially with all that reverb, so I'm determined to make the most of it. If I'm enjoying the song, I will give it energy, and if it has energy then it will be fab! I've really thought about the words, and the song runs a nice cycle. I think it could potentially be great. My only worry is my starting note but I'm sure it'll be OK. I'll be thinking about Karen beforehand and I know that will help.

WEDNESDAY, 21 NOVEMBER 2001

I was up by 6.30 and left the hotel by 8. Got to the studios and had a quick warm-up with Mike, who just cracks me up. I had a couple of group interviews with Kate but they didn't go as well as yesterday as I didn't say much – I just kept thinking about Karen. Kate said I was kind of a Hugh Grant, a bumbling figure. I'm not sure whether that's a good image or not!

Anyway, as it happens it wasn't my dance moves that let me down, it was (surprise surprise) my mouth! Once again, I was last to go out to face the judges and I'd been sitting in that Green Room for ages, watching the other nine contestants singing. They were all fantastic but some of the judges' comments were a bit harsh. Actually, some of the stuff Cowell said to people was awful – it really made me angry. Here was his chance to give constructive criticism and he decided to insult people instead.

So anyway it was my turn to go out and even if I do say so myself it was a bloody good performance. When I'd finished I could hear all the others going crazy in the Green Room. But what did the judges say?

Pete: 'At last, at least you gave it your best shot. I think you were more enthusiastic, I thought you tried to do something different. You did wake me up and I thank you for that.'

Brilliant!

Nicki: 'Great, great version and for us a brilliant way to end seeing all ten. I thought it was exceptional and I really, really liked it. Well done.'

Fab!

Foxy: 'You improved your game in the second half by owning the song and doing your own version which is really important because to cover a record you've got to put your own stamp on it. I wonder whether you are the pop idol but as a singer you're cracking!'

Hmm, didn't know whether or not to take that as a compliment. But then...

Simon: 'Erm, William, this is where I put a shield up against you three. I had a vision of Sunday lunch and after Sunday lunch you say to your family, "I'm now going to sing a song for you." Distinctly average, I'm afraid.'

I tell you, I was so shocked because I know from everything that Mike, Carrie, David and Marianne have said that my performance wasn't average. I just had to ask him to elaborate...

'I just thought it was totally normal – in the context of this show I honestly didn't think it was good enough.'

I just thought, Bloody hell, BLOODY HELL! That is exactly what was running through my head and I thought, That's it, it's over.

Then Nicki says, 'Please don't take that, please say something back.'

Thank you so much, Nicki – don't ask me where it came from but I suddenly burst out with, 'I love disagreeing with Simon cos I do it every week but all of us have been dying to say things to you –'

Simon: 'Well, I just spoke how I felt so –'

How dare he interrupt me? I was livid!

'Sorry, can I finish? Thank you.' Very proud of that bit! 'I think it's nice that you have given opinions in this show. I think in previous shows you haven't, you've just given projected insults and it's been terrible to watch. I think this show you have been better and I think you have given opinions and I think you backed up your opinions, which the other three do, which is what I respect. It *is* your opinion but I don't agree with it. I don't think it was average. I don't think you could ever call that average, but it is your opinion and I respect that so thank you very much.'

And as I waited for another tongue-lashing, he simply replied, 'You are a gentleman, sir.'

I walked off that stage shaking like a leaf – I'm not normally one for outbursts but if something has got to be said then I'll say it. As I made my way back to the Green Room where everybody was whooping and shrieking at my outburst, I couldn't believe what I'd just done. I remember saying to Ant and Dec, 'It was nice of Nicki to stand up for me because I think I would have just walked away otherwise.' I know my father would have been going, 'You're not taking that my boy, Annabel, get the shotgun!'

Ant and Dec were brilliant and praised me for what I said, and I must admit I had the biggest grin ever on my face. I was petrified that I'd blown it but so pleased I didn't let him bully me and I really think I managed to put him in his place. I didn't want to speak to him after that but we had a little conversation when we were retaking the final walk-out, when I said, 'I can work most people out, but you are a mystery.' I could see him wanting to talk and relieve his embarrassment but I didn't want to give him the opportunity! I did shake his hand, and of course I was polite, but I still stood and stand by what I said – definitely.

You know what, though – I cared far more about what the rest of the guys in the Green Room thought. They are my fellow competitors and to have earned their respect was far more rewarding. I'll never forget the feeling of walking into the Green Room and everyone cheering – it was just amazing. I felt like a hero. It's a great feeling that just being you does actually appeal to people. Maybe I can make it in this industry just being me! I promise myself now I will NEVER compromise who I am.

It's also made me realise that this is something that I'm really passionate about. Suddenly it doesn't seem like some idealistic dream but is something more real and attainable. I really do believe that I can do it – I know I've got what it takes and it's just down to chance or luck and all that nonsense. When the music really touches my heart and soul it makes all the difference. That's what it's been like the last three days.

All we have to do now is wait for the results but that isn't until Saturday... This is a very cruel show.

THURSDAY, 22 NOVEMBER 2001

I woke up this morning and I know it's really naughty but I couldn't handle going to college (listen to me – I sound like a school child!). I called up and told them that I had a migraine, then I pottered around and did lots of bits. Went for a lovely walk in Hyde Park, chilled out at home and then watched *Pop Idol Extra* until about 2.30 in the morning! This is all so weird – one minute performing on TV and the next back to being a student. Everyone at college has found out that I'm on the show this week and that means they're all going to be watching – oh my God!

FRIDAY, 23 NOVEMBER 2001

Not the nicest day ever. It was Karen's funeral and I was running late. Jumped in a taxi to Paddington, then onto the train to Heathrow where I met Mum, Rupert and Emma. Got the plane up to Dundee where Dad met us and we drove to a grim pub for a drink (and I do really mean grim). The funeral was, well, a funeral, and today the world has lost a wonderful person.

SATURDAY, 24 NOVEMBER 2001

Arrived back from Dundee late last night and really didn't want to go to the studio today. I felt really deflated but I know Karen would have wanted me to go on. Arrived in the afternoon, got made up, had a run-through and dress rehearsal with Ant and Dec and then it was time for the show. We watched it at the TV studios (which was very strange, I have to say) and then we had two hours to wait before the show came back on air for the results. My nerves were in shreds – in fact the smoking has got out of control – far too many a day. Note to self: must try and give it up!

But there was no point in being nervous because I gave it my best shot – but did I think it was good enough to get through? That thought had been in my mind all night. I was pleased with my performance when I watched it but I thought Korben did extremely well, too. Then came the results – in fifth place, Rebecca, fourth place, Tania, then Natalie… three down, two more to choose. Then they said 'Korben' and I honestly thought it was all over there and then. Then they said 'in first place... Will Young.' I was speechless – it was an incredible moment. Amazing! I would have been really upset if I hadn't got in the top five but I'd never really thought about my name being called out in first or second place. Katie was with me tonight and she was so happy for me. We decided to go out afterwards and meet up with loads of friends at a club in Clapham. What a night it's been – so nice to see everybody and they were all so excited for me!

So I'm up against Gareth, Zoe, Hayley, Laura, Rosie and Jessica and Korben. Another two to go and then we have the final ten. Wish me luck!

SUNDAY, 25 NOVEMBER 2001

Eurgh, my head still hurts! Was working with Ray Monk (the guy replacing Mike Dixon as he is now musical director of the new Queen musical – knew he was talented!) today busy routining the first two songs that we have to have ready for the final ten. The two songs I've chosen are Aretha Franklin's 'Until You Come Back To Me' – which I'll perform on the first show of the final ten – and then if I make it to the next round I'll be singing 'Winter Wonderland'. We've been given themes for the live shows and we get to choose the songs. So the first week is songs by your pop idol (thus an Aretha song – I know I put Tina Turner was my idol on my application form but I love Aretha as well and her songs are just brilliant to sing) and the next week is Christmas songs. It's all getting very exciting now but I don't think I'll appreciate quite how thrilling it is until I'm on the first show and doing it! We've just been told that the first round will be shown live… yes, that's LIVE, on 15 December – oh my God!

MONDAY, 26 NOVEMBER 2001

Korben and I had to be interviewed by Eamonn Holmes on *GMTV* this morning – how funny is that? I don't really know Korben that well but he's quite an extrovert – which is good because it meant I didn't have to say much! We were there to talk about us being the next two to get through – all the contestants who have so far got through to the final ten have done it. It was a great interview and of course more live telly, but my first thought wasn't what I was going to say but that the studio looks much bigger when you're watching it on the television at home! Then we had to pop in for a quick chat with the lovely Lorraine Kelly – that was a lot of fun. I've had a right laugh over the last week but it's back to reality and off to college for me tomorrow!

FRIDAY 7 DECEMBER, 2001

Last day of college today. Sorry I haven't written for a while! I've had so many assessments to do it's ridiculous (who'd have thought I would know so much about the history of dance!). I've even had to be an Aborigine in a play and all I had to wear for that was a loincloth! Very strange, let me tell you – definitely not something to be seen out on the town in! It's been three weeks since my last show on the telly and I have to admit I am raring to go. It's been very strange not being near a TV studio but it's probably a good thing because I'm really trying to concentrate on my studies. *Pop Idol*'s about to kick off so I'm making the most of being able to write to you now – God knows if I'll have time next week. The line-up was completed last Saturday and I watched it on video last night (well, I have got a social life – I can't stay in and watch every show). I really thought it was a tough week, too, because it seems to me there were four people that should have gone through. Aaron Bayley, Rik Waller, Darius Danesh (no, seriously, he was good!) and Sarah

Whatmore. Personally I thought it was between Sarah and Rik but Aaron (singing 'Walking In Memphis') and Rik (who sang an impressive 'I Can't Make You Love Me') were chosen. They've both got unique voices – I'm going to have my work cut out!

MONDAY, 10 DECEMBER 2001

Met up with the nine other contestants today! They are Rosie Ribbons, Aaron Bayley, Rik Waller, Gareth Gates, Zoe Birkett, Jessica Garlick, Laura Doherty, Korben and Hayley Evetts – and they're all really lovely. We're all so excited at getting this far I don't think any of us have really thought about what we're letting ourselves in for! We're being put up in the Marriott Hotel in Maida Vale AND we're being given £150 a week for expenses – clothes, travel, just basic living, really, which is cool – at least we can all get by! Had a photo shoot with *OK!* today as well – get us! But to be honest I wasn't in the mood today, and neither was Rosie. We both met out on the patio of this amazing flat where we were doing the shoot and just looked so fed up – so I lit up a fag and we both had a moan. We weren't being ungrateful but both of us were really down – no particular reason but it was good to have each other to get it off our chests. Rosie seems lovely. It was a great day all in all – we all felt like models. Gareth and Zoe were like two kids who had the run of a sweet shop and Hayley looked sensational. We've got used to getting our make-up done for the TV show and today was no exception because not only were we having our photographs taken but we were being filmed for the TV show, too. Not too many people in one room then!

The photographer was called Nicky Johnston – very well respected in this industry apparently. I can see why – he's very good at his job, especially as he got lumbered with a bunch of people who had never done modelling before or even had their photo taken professionally. He told us how to look at the camera, what to do with our hands (I never know what to do with my hands when I'm performing) and to hold our heads at certain angles cos we looked better. He was brilliant!

The journalist from the magazine interviewed us, too – everybody seemed so nice and I could quite get used to this way of life! I was in a much better mood by the time we finished. Then it was back to the hotel for a quick beer and a chat with the others.

TUESDAY, 11 DECEMBER 2001

Had a press conference today for the final ten – so many people and cameras! I thought it would be scary to be facing that many journalists who want to know everything about us. But it wasn't too bad at all – in fact apart from having to describe ourselves to the assorted press the only thing I was asked was, 'What if you win and you don't get any say in things that you release?' I just replied, 'If I was to win then people will, by that stage, know my style of music and I would imagine that people around us musically will think of songs set around that kind of style.' And when that was finally over, we had to go for an interview with the Disney Channel. It really does seem to becoming reality now – our schedules are packed to the brim with promotion, filming and rehearsals for the show.

THURSDAY, 13 DECEMBER 2001

Had our vocal training with David, Carrie and Mike today – they are amazing. So full of encouragement and wise words – we're very lucky to have such talented people working with us. I know I've still got so much to learn so I've been listening to them and taking their advice on board – they've helped me feel comfortable with my voice and how I sing. But there's still plenty of room for improvement!

FRIDAY, 14 DECEMBER 2001

This morning was so weird! We all went off to be interviewed on *This Morning* and I had the strangest *déjà vu* – it's where we did that boy-band competition all those years ago!

After that it was off to the Fountain Studios in Wembley, which is where our debut live show will be held. It was the first time we'd seen the official *Pop Idol* set – it's massive, it really is, and of course there's loads of seating because tomorrow we'll actually be performing to an audience of 500 in the studio. But if I start to think about that I'll be all over the place so first stop was my clothes – v. important! After many discussions with Toni, Tony and Nicole (the stylists) I settled on baggy trousers, chequered tank top and trainers. Cool but casual and more importantly, comfy!! Then we had technical rehearsals at about 5pm – we all got about three turns on the mike just to check out the sound. But do you know what? It was the scariest moment for me because I could see what everybody else in this final was capable of. Korben sounded great and so did Rosie, but I was such a nervous wreck – I lost count of how many times I asked if it sounded alright.

SATURDAY, 15 DECEMBER 2001

Oh my god! It's the first live TV show today and I was quite calm and scared at the same time – kind of like judgement day had arrived, the prisoner resigned to his execution. Before I went to the studios I decided to pop home quickly to grab a few things. It was about 8am and I left my car for literally two minutes and when I got back outside it was being towed away. I couldn't believe it was happening but I couldn't help laughing – I even waved goodbye to my car as it was carried off into the distance. Well, there was nothing I could do – I had to get to the studios in an hour.

The theme tonight was song to sing by your favourite pop idol and I chose Aretha Frankin and her marvellous song 'Until You Come Back To Me'. All the other songs were great, too…

Jessica sang 'Papa Don't Preach' by Madonna
Korben chose 'A Different Corner' by George Michael
Gareth sang 'Everything I Do' by Bryan Adams

Zoe went for 'I Will Always Love You' by Whitney Houston

Laura plumped for 'She's Out Of My Life' by Michael Jackson

Hayley decided on 'Made For Lovin' You' by Anastacia

Aaron performed 'Jesus To A Child' by George Michael

Rosie chose 'Whenever You Call' by Mariah Carey

(One of the contestants, Rik Waller, was ill with a sore throat and couldn't even perform. How pissed off would you be if you'd got this far and that happened? I didn't really know him to be honest, because he's been ill this last week, but I felt sorry for the bloke!)

So several run-throughs and a dress rehearsal later (which we found out they filmed to use in the re-run bit just after we performed – very clever!), it was time for the final make-up checks before waiting backstage to be called. The nerves were starting to kick in with everyone, and then before we knew it we were being introduced on stage, one by one. I was just keeping myself to myself and trying not to think about anything at all – particularly the audience or the fact that somebody was going to be voted out. I didn't watch the performances because I like to have my own space and chill. They've changed all the voting around, though, because it was going to be that the public had to vote for whoever they thought was the worst and now we've been told that they vote for whoever they think is the best. The person with the least number of votes goes!

So I walked out on stage, head down, and then as I started the song I was trying not to look into the audience because I would have been looking for Rupert and Emma. Then the audience started clapping along to the song, which completely stopped me from searching for anyone. Apart from messing it up at the beginning where my voice sounded like it was trying to break (which was awful), the performance was good.

Then it was over and I turned to the judges. My stomach was churning. Foxy was first up...

Foxy: 'You always do really well in the second half of your performance but I've got a few marks for you. Jumper 2/10. (Cheek! Have you looked in the mirror at some of your suits recently, Foxy?) Voice 8/10. Personality 10/10.'

Nicki: 'William, you are a gentleman, it has to be said, and I think you really raised the mood here tonight. Every time you perform you make it your own. It's your own version of that song and for me it really, really works. Well done!'

Pete: 'Will, what are you going to say, with the nation sitting there breathless? I actually think you have the most unique voice I've heard in twenty years. Simon and I just sat here and said, "This kid is fantastic." You just do the songs your own way – you're fantastic.'

Wow – what do you say to that?

Simon: 'William, first question, has your dad got his shot-gun with him? I have to say, William, you more than anyone else humbled me from the last time. I watched it back and I realised I made a huge mistake with what I said and I thought the way you handled yourself was with dignity.'

I was worried about what he was going to say after my outburst but he was so nice! It means a lot that he's backed down.

Simon: 'And this is what makes the competition so fantastic because the public voted against Big Mouth and I'm delighted for you. You did brilliant. Congratulations.'

Blimey – even Ant and Dec were gobsmacked that I got an apology from Simon Cowell. And I can't believe that Pete said I had the most unique voice he'd heard in twenty years – what an accolade. My head was all over the place as I came offstage, so I disappeared into a dressing room to calm myself down. Didn't have too much time to think about how the voting would go because as soon as *Pop Idol* finished on ITV1, Kate Thornton was ready in the wings to take over for ITV2, which went on until the results. It was nice that we could all have a chat with Kate, but as the time ticked by you could feel the initial nerves coming back. Somebody would be leaving tonight – I really didn't have a clue who because I thought we were all brilliant.

As if we weren't nervous enough, Declan Donnelly dropped me right in it live on the show! He announced that my car had been towed away – which would have been fine except my family didn't know! Well, they definitely found out tonight cos he exposed me live on national television, the sod! It was very funny though.

And then... the judges' predictions!

Foxy – Laura

Nicki – Laura

Pete – Korben

Simon – Laura

Like I say, I didn't think any of us should have gone tonight but I didn't agree with the judges' choice. More importantly, though, we were about to find out what the public thought...

Jessica was, surprisingly, the first on the couch, then it was me – but I was safe! Oh, the relief that ran through my body! Then Korben was called to the couch, with Hayley, Zoe, Aaron, Gareth and Rosie all remaining safe. It ended up with Jessica, Korben and Laura on the couch but it was Korben who was going. I was shocked because I really thought Korben was in with a chance to go all the way to the final. He looked brilliant and he sounded great but the audience obviously didn't think the same. It was sad to see him go – well, we were all a bit gloomy because we had just lost the first group member. Hope it doesn't feel this bad every week! Then after the show we were all back to talk to Kate for ITV2 – and Korben just looked devastated. It was hard to feel happy when we'd got through and he hadn't.

SUNDAY, 16 DECEMBER 2001

I had to go and pick my car up this morning. If I couldn't just jump into that and drive wherever I wanted I think I'd go mad! Walked into the car pound's portacabin and told the woman behind the desk I was there to collect my red Ferrari. She just looked at me and said, 'Pull the other one!' Think everyone there must have heard that joke more than once! But the most hilarious thing for me was that they had seen me on the show last night (I keep forgetting that I'm on the telly and that people might recognise me!) and they told me that Simon Cowell's car had been in the week before – which made me very happy, as you can imagine!

Met up with Ray and routined out our next group of songs – the theme for the third show is going to be music by Burt Bacharach and I'm very excited because his songs are genius. Mind you, that's if I get that far – it's very strange practising for songs we might not get to sing. I've chosen 'Wives And Lovers' but at the moment I can't wait until this Saturday because I'll be singing 'Winter Wonderland' for the Christmas show – I love that song. Have decided to slow it down but seriously jazz it up. Can't wait to perform it!

MONDAY, 17 DECEMBER 2001

The press office are keen for everyone to have the same amount of time in front of the press so we have to be very careful because there are journalists and photographers hanging around the hotel we're staying in. Me and Hayley have really bonded this week and when we went out for a drink today there were photographers everywhere and lights flashing in our faces – is this what it's going to be like? It was very strange and it did make me wonder about fame – oh dear I think *Pop Idol* might be huge!

WEDNESDAY, 19 DECEMBER 2001

I had such a fun day today. We were all given £10 and had
to buy a Christmas present for one of the others. I drew
Aaron, which was great because he's such a laugh. I went to
a shopping centre in Watford with Rosie (and a TV crew in
tow – hardly inconspicuous!) and searched everywhere for
something suitable. Ended up buying him a silver Elvis and
beer socks – definitely very Aaron!

THURSDAY, 20 DECEMBER 2001

It was a very strange rehearsal for us because we were told that Rik will probably be leaving if his throat isn't better by tomorrow, and although most of us don't know him that well it would be sad to see him leave. But what's strange is that Darius has been brought in today to replace him! When I found out that Rik might be leaving I instantly thought, Why not get the person who was voted out in the first programme back in and start afresh? However, Darius was the next runner up out of the forty, so that was fair. It was strange at first but by the end of the day it was like he'd always been with us. Must be weird for him, though – he doesn't know if he'll definitely be on the show yet.

It's going to be a good show on Saturday – I could feel it in rehearsals. Everybody was in a festive mood today and the songs we're singing on Saturday will make the night go with a bang...

Hayley – 'Rockin' Around The Christmas Tree' – brilliant

Gareth – 'Last Christmas' – thumbs aloft everybody

Jessica – 'Merry Christmas Everyone'– sums up
   Christmas for me!

Aaron – 'I'm Dreaming Of A White Christmas' – classic

Rosie – 'Santa Baby' – saucy!

Laura – 'I Wish It Could Be Christmas' – pure Christmas

Darius – 'When A Child Is Born' – class

Zoe – 'All I Want For Christmas' – bring it on!

SATURDAY, 22 DECEMBER 2001

I couldn't wait to get on that stage and perform 'Winter Wonderland'. We found out that Rik definitely wouldn't be with us for this show and that Darius was in. So after all the usual technical rehearsals, dress rehearsals, make-up rehearsals (only joking!), we were on schedule for another great show – except this time Korben wouldn't be with us.

In the Green Room we gave each other our £10 presents...

Gareth bought Rosie false nails, stick-on jewels and
    hair clips.
Jessica bought Darius an Ali G beard and a Britney
    calendar.
Aaron got Hayley a Tigger.
Rosie bought Zoe a yellow space hopper.
Laura bought Jessica a pink sparkly top.
Darius got Laura a pen engraved with her name
    and 'Keep smiling' on it.
Zoe got Gareth an S Club 7 calendar!

'Meeting the public!'

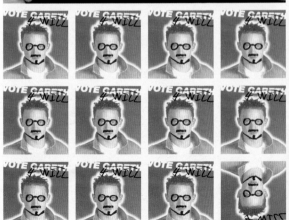

'Yes of course I get
on really well with Gareth!'

'This Morning' – always a laugh.'

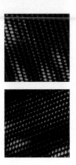

'Ant & Dec – top blokes!'
'The final – us, nervous?!' _ opposite

'Come on baby, light my fire!'

'The final performance.'

'The winning moment.'

And Hayley got lumbered with me and bought me
   a very cool hat and two toy cars to replace the
   one that got towed away! Ha ha, very funny,
   Hayley Bayley!

Then it was time to get back down to business. I'd decided
on wearing a black see-through shirt, trousers and shoes
this week – wanted to be a bit smarter for this one. I felt
really smooth in them. Carole, one of the make-up artists,
gave me something to think of when I was on stage. For
Aretha Franklin she had said Funky Chicken and for this
one it was Crooning Skunk – it sounds funny but it got me
into character for the song. I waited backstage to go on and
then they called my name – here we go! Tried not to look out
into the audience for Rupert and Emma and the rest of my
motley crew. Walked on stage and the audience was going
wild – it was such a fantastic atmosphere! Sat on the stool
and belted out 'Winter Wonderland' and I was very, very
pleased with my performance. I turned to the judges, minus
Simon Cowell who was off sunning himself somewhere,
thank God!

Pete: 'Well, I said it all last week, didn't I? You made me
a hero! You really have got a great voice and I could sit here
and listen to you singing all day. You can never predict how
you're going to sing a song. You sing it beautifully and then
you go into it. I've been trying to think all week of who you
remind me of and it's Bobby Darin, and a few people will

know he could have followed Sinatra but unfortunately he didn't live long enough. I think you have a Sinatra-esque quality about your voice. It's different.'

Yeeeeeessss – but who's Bobby Darin?

Nicki: 'It's an absolute joy to sit here and watch you perform. There's a real swing about your performance. Looking back to the early days of these auditions, I struggle to remember you, but since filming at Teddington, you really have been up there and you've really raised the stakes.'

Foxy: 'I thought you were brilliant tonight. You remind me, in the way you sing, of Mick Hucknall. He sings so effortlessly on stage and you have that relaxing quality in your eye. You looked like you were loving it. I could listen to you all day, I really could. Well done.'

How spooky – my uncle had sent me a message saying, 'I know who you remind me of… Mick Hucknall,' and now Foxy reckons that's who I remind him of. Cool! I love Simply Red's *Picturebook* album.

But as is the norm on a Saturday we had to wait for the results… ITV2 didn't know what had hit them. We were all so nervous but it was such a wonderful atmosphere at the studios because it was the last show before Christmas. We had so much fun but secretly, deep down, we were all bricking it.

The judges were still undecided on who they thought would go:

Nicki – Jessica

Pete – Laura

Foxy – Jessica

The results came in and Laura, Rosie and Jessica were on the Couch of Cruelty (as it's now been dubbed). I really didn't know who was going to leave out of the three. Laura and Jessica had already been on the couch once and tonight it was Jessica that was the one to leave. Very sad! But it didn't stop her partying at the *Pop Idol* Christmas party, which took place in the glamorous location of – the bar backstage! I managed to sneak in some extra guests and my friends just took over. There was Emma, Hugh, Chappell, Rupert, Pilky, Milsy and Andy D all going for it! It was one of the nicest nights I've ever had – cheesy songs, the *Pop Idol* team and all my friends. A perfect night out! Claire the producer did her party piece – as Lulu in the Take That version of 'Relight My Fire' – absolutely hilarious. Ant and Dec did a special performance of 'Let's Get Ready To Rumble' and me, Gareth, Zoe and Hayley just had a dance around. Then before I knew it Hugh had started a conga around the room – it's so nice to have friends you don't need to worry about and can enjoy themselves. The party finished at 3am and I came back to the hotel. A good day's work!

SUNDAY, 23 DECEMBER 2001

Was absolutely knackered but luckily didn't have too much to do today – we just routined for the show after next. The theme is music from the movies. Have thought about this a lot and decided to go for 'Shake Your Tail Feathers' from *The Blues Brothers* – it's such a great song and the film is bloody funny. We've officially broken up from *Pop Idol* for Christmas – hooray! I cannot wait for Christmas Day, though I must say it will be very strange not seeing the others for the next four or five days!

MONDAY, 24 DECEMBER 2001

Went down to Bath to see Adam and do my Christmas shopping. I've only got today to do it so I've GOT to get it all done. It was funny though because I didn't get recognised at all, which was great, but Adam did! He may have been one of my best friends for ever, but he's an actor in his own right. People say that you should drop your friends if they become more famous than you and I can see why – only joking, Adam! Got the shopping done in the few hours that I had. (A record!) I was absolutely shattered but managed to drive back home to Mum and Dad's house and then I popped out for a quick drink.

THURSDAY, 27 DECEMBER 2001

Sorry I haven't written but I only had three days off and I had so much to do and so many people to see! Came back to London yesterday after a wonderful family Christmas – had a really great time and it was so nice to catch up with friends and family. We've been rehearsing today and I have to be honest, I'm finding 'Wives And Lovers' a very difficult song to sing. But it has such a great beginning which hopefully will grab the attention of the audience. Wish I'd chosen 'Walk On By' now cos that's one of my favourite songs and nobody else has chosen it but this is what we're all going to sing tomorrow…

Aaron – 'Twenty-Four Hours From Tulsa'

Zoe – 'Say A Little Prayer'

Gareth – 'Arthur's Theme'

Laura – 'Always Something There To Remind Me'

Rosie – 'That's What Friends Are For'

Darius – 'What The World Needs Now'

Hayley – 'Do You Know The Way To San Jose?'

SATURDAY, 29 DECEMBER 2002

I can't believe Christmas is over already. It always goes so fast. Ah, well, at least we've still got New Year's Eve to party away, even though I still don't know what I'm doing.

Found a great suit for this show – a fantastic maroon pinstripe suit (a bargain at £60 from Top Man!) with a beige shirt. I wanted to go smart but cool for the Burt Bacharach – very seventies. Toni and Nicole know my style by now and they did very well with this outfit, I must say.

They showed the *OK!* photo shoot on the programme today – I caught a glimpse on one of the monitors backstage and it looked hilarious. Still not watching anyone perform – I'm much more at ease on my own and concentrating on what I'm going to be doing. The last thing I need to be worrying about is whether one of the others is doing better than me!

Thought I was actually a bit off-key tonight. I really wasn't with it and I think it must have been because I'd just come back from my Christmas celebrations. Even the audience was a bit strange – there wasn't a good vibe out there at all. Very bizarre! I enjoyed the song but I was glad when it was over. Mum finally made it to one of the shows, but it's typical that the one she chose to come to wasn't the usual upbeat party fun! Oh well, can't have it all, I suppose! Then it was judgment time…

Nicki: 'Each week you get stronger and stronger. I still don't remember you at the beginning of this search and now look at you, each week you come on. I don't know what made you choose that track. Is it a favourite? It suits you so well, though. Well done.'

Cool!

Foxy: 'William, I think you are pure class when you sing. You love singing and it's so easy to watch you and it's such a lovely thing. I think you could become the new young king of cool. Robbie Williams has the biggest-selling album this year with *Swing When You're Winning*. You could have done that album. You could do Burt Bacharach covers and it would sell millions because you do it really well. I think you're going to go a long way.'

Oh my God!

Pete: 'Do you want the good news or the bad news? The bad news is that you're not a pop idol…You're a superstar!'

I'm just absolutely loving it and I'm kind of waiting – and I know this is pessimistic – for the fall every week. But I feel so comfortable out there on stage!

We had two hours to wait before this week's results.

Arrggghhh, this is driving me bonkers and it's getting harder every week because the longer we're together the closer we become. Losing someone every week is getting so hard.

This week the judges went for:

Nicki – Rosie
Pete – Aaron
Foxy – Rosie

Laura, Rosie and Aaron were on the couch this week and unfortunately it was Aaron's turn to leave us – didn't see that one coming, but then I haven't guessed right once yet! Losing Aaron is a real shame because the group will suffer for him leaving. He always diffused any dodgy situations with a joke so we're all going to miss him. But he was very calm – he knows that it is just the nature of the competition. No one goes because they aren't good enough. I think we all take comfort from that.

After the show it was all back to the hotel to drown Aaron's sorrows!

SUNDAY, 30 DECEMBER 2001

Routined the song for the movie theme week today – wasn't massively happy with it but I thought once I'd spoken to David and Carrie I'd be OK for the show. Went back to the flat and I know this is going to sound like I'm mad but I had a really deep thought when I was in the shower and 'Ain't No Sunshine' came into my head. There I was singing it in the shower and I started to cry. I just thought, that's a really sad song, and realised it was from the film *Notting Hill*. Decided that I needed another confident performance. I'd done two crooners and I really did need another boost. I phoned Ray Monk to see if it was too late to change my song and whether or not he'd sent the music to the orchestra yet. He hadn't and told me to get down to his studio first thing tomorrow morning to get everything changed.

MONDAY, 31 DECEMBER 2001

Got to Ray's first thing and routined 'Ain't No Sunshine'. I'm so happy I was able to change my song – I feel much more comfortable singing this. Raced back into town because we had a photo shoot with a newspaper and, as usual, I was running late and all the other contestants were waiting for me – ooops! Have decided to work at a party tonight as a barman. I think it'll do me good to get out and about – normal world here I come!

WEDNESDAY, 2 JANUARY 2002

I cannot believe New Year's Eve has been and gone. It was nice to do some normal work for a change I obviously needed a bit of normality in my life and the pay wasn't bad either so I thought, Why not?

Today we all went to Pete Waterman's studio on one of our daily excursions and it was great fun – walked into the reception and it was wall-to-wall mounted discs. I looked around and hadn't heard of half the bands whose names were engraved on them but it looked bloody impressive! I'd never been to a recording studio before so I was quite nervous (but very excited) and I suddenly realised I was somewhere I had always wanted to be. It was quite an emotional moment – I was shaking. I went into the soundproof room to sing and just felt so at home – we did it in one take, which Pete said was amazing! It felt so right to be in there and I would love to work with him – it would be cool to see him in his role as producer rather than judge. We chose our songs for an Abba night and a big-band night as well today

– I think I'm going for 'The Name Of The Game' for Abba (which we'll do next week) and 'We Are In Love' by Harry Connick Jr for the week after. I hadn't heard the Harry Connick Jr song before today but when I did I just thought, Yes, that's the one! But hey, who knows, maybe I'll change my mind again or even worse maybe I won't make it to either of those weeks! I bloody hope so though because I've worked extremely hard to get where I am and I've always wanted to sing with a big band.

THURSDAY, 3 JANUARY 2002

We're down to seven now and it's really strange because we're turning up for things and wondering where everybody else is. Went through the dynamics for 'Ain't No Sunshine' with David and Carrie today and between us we changed a few notes here and there. We had the entire song down to a T by the end of the day – incredible!

FRIDAY, 4 JANUARY 2002

Had the usual rehearsals today and it sounded wicked. Went through my clothes with the styling team and we decided to keep it simple – black leather jacket, red T-shirt, blue jeans and white trainers. It looked cool. Even Carrie came up to me and said, 'You look like a pop star.' Let's just hope the public like it, too!

SATURDAY, 5 JANUARY 2002

Didn't have a good dress rehearsal today because I felt a bit out of sorts. I don't know if it's because the song moves me so much or that I really need the pressure and the adrenalin to perform well. Maybe it's a mixture of both? Carrie was watching the rehearsal and just came up to me and said, 'Just bloody sing it – go out there and do it.' Carrie never swears but she bucked my ideas up, that's for sure! My father came to the show today, which was great, but it didn't help that the song is one of his favourites. But I really needed something else to help me tune into this song and today I thought of Karen – our very dear friend who died last year. I reckon she was looking down at me thinking, cheap trick for a competition, Will!

I felt better by the time I was ready to go out on stage. Pop star outfit on, make-up done, I just thought, Watch out, world, here I come!!!

The audience was electric – there was such a buzz as I walked out on stage, it was amazing. I just lost myself in that performance. I was completely shaking after I'd finished – my eyes were filled with tears. Foxy was away this week which meant that Simon Cowell was back. I had to take a big deep breath before I turned to the judges and then I tripped in front of everybody! I was just hoping that nobody noticed. Would Simon be more chilled out if he'd been on holiday? I was about to find out.

Simon: 'First question: where's your dad?'

'He's behind you,' I replied coolly.

Simon: 'You're like a racehorse, you are, Will. You just trot along at the beginning of the song, doing not much and then, bang, you race. It's always the same – you're fantastic at the end of your songs.'

Blimey – a holiday obviously did him good!

Pete: 'I think you do alright at the start. That song does suit your voice. You sing it equally as good as Bill Withers does. That's your sort of song.'

Nicki: 'Pete's right. You always pick the right song for you when you perform, and we talk about the pop idol or the person to entertain us and it's a whole package, not just about the voice, it's everything, and you really do deliver. We're paying you compliments and I don't think it's going to your head. You're still going to remain the same, Will, so keep going, because you're getting it right!'

Wow, they liked it, and although I was elated I was equally exhausted after my performance. Carrie and David came up to me afterwards and said, 'You've just had your first moment on stage.' Which I think was true. You've got to have an emotional link with whatever you are doing – a great lesson I learnt at college. When you approach a song you have to get a moment when you emotionally identify with it and that is the moment when you should burst into tears, which is exactly what I did the time I thought of it in the shower – thank you, Karen xx

We waited for the results – same old same old. But this week was the first time that the judges actually agreed on who would go… they all went for Laura. She had been on the couch THREE times – how dejected must she have been feeling? She came out week after week fighting and she really went for it, but sadly this week she lost out. I think she had had enough – not that you could see that from her perform-ance. Shame she had to go.

Went back to Tom's flat and just chilled out with him, Emma and a few others. Nice!

SUNDAY, 6 JANUARY 2002

Today Hayley, Darius, Gareth, Zoe, Rosie and me all went to a very posh health farm – Hanbury Manor, if you don't mind! I was so hungover this morning the last thing I needed was a day of filming for the show, but I had to be professional and being taken to a health farm isn't so bad! Having said that, it wasn't exactly relaxing. It had to look like we had all this time being pampered when really we just had to do all this filming. Did some interviews, then we did some dancing with choreographer Paul Roberts in the afternoon. I felt really confident thanks to college – I've only been there five weeks but I've had lots of time practising in dance studios. Paul's assistant was lovely and they both really helped us out, but I was quite chuffed when Paul said that I was the best out of the boys – not bad with the hang-over from hell! Then had another interview to do for the TV show. I don't mind doing the interviews but we could do twenty different ones for a single show and possibly only one might be used. It's very disheartening. Actually TV is the most knackering thing – it's so tiring, particularly with all the takes that we do.

Met for dinner about seven o'clock and then we had more filming to do. They made the six of us sit round this roaring open fire with these hilarious dressing gowns on and we were sweating buckets – hopefully you won't see that on camera! The scene was set up but everything we were saying was honest and genuine and more than anything it was actually really nice just to catch up and chat to each other normally. Everyone's lovely and we really are all very supportive of each other – since there were only ten of us it has never been about rivalry. I suppose underneath we *are* all looking out for number one but what's the point of being rivals? Didn't finish filming until about 12.30am and I'm now knackered so I'm off to bed!

MONDAY, 7 JANUARY 2002

Got up early this morning – we had loads more filming to do and I had to go and play golf! I wasn't bad considering it's Rupert who's the golfer in our family. I learnt a lot which was cool. I might play again in the future – hey, maybe I'll take some lessons and then I can give Rupert a run for his money. Then Gareth and I had to play tennis – he's such a good sportsman (he was brilliant at golf) but I'm pleased to say that I held my own on the court. Which is just as well because I lied and told the TV show that I used to play tennis for my county – ha ha! Oh well, if you can't tell a little fib every now and again life would be very boring indeed!

TUESDAY, 8 JANUARY 2002

We have been told today that because there aren't many of us now, we will be leaving our respective hotel rooms and moving into a suite. Hurray! Well, all of us except Gareth and Zoe – they get a suite for themselves and their parents because they're both under eighteen! So tomorrow Darius, Hayley, Rosie and I will officially be suite-mates. It'll be so nice to have a communal area to chill out in together – a hotel room can be a very lonely place.

WEDNESDAY, 9 JANUARY 2002

I name this suite 'Pop Idol Hell'. Ha ha! It is so nice – it's got a washing machine, kitchen, sitting room… It's so much better than just a room in a hotel. It's not home but it certainly feels one step closer! So today has been spent moving into our rooms and checking out all the new gadgets! I suppose it will be strange sharing with people I've only known for a few weeks. I've already discovered Darius's worst habit… SINGING constantly! As if we don't do enough of that already!

THURSDAY, 10 JANUARY 2002

Back on track today which means working with David
and Carrie on our songs. It's the Abba show on Saturday
and I'm going to be singing 'The Name Of The Game' –
I've only chosen this one because I couldn't get to grips
with any of the others. Have routined the song with
David and Carrie and I'm still not sure about it but it's too
late to change now and also this is the nearest Abba ever
got to soul – it's got that brilliant beginning. Everybody
is feeling a bit funny about this whole Abba week – it's
the first week where we've all felt that we can't rise to
the occasion. Who'd have thought Abba songs were so
incredibly difficult for me to sing? I think I've got the best
out of a bad bunch!

Anyway these are the ones that we've chosen…

Hayley – 'Take A Chance'
Darius – 'I Have A Dream'
Rosie – 'The Winner Takes It All'

Gareth – 'One Of Us'

Zoe – 'Thank You For The Music'

FRIDAY, 11 JANUARY 2002

This morning we had a photo shoot with *Now* magazine –
we had to get all dressed up in these hilarious big-band type
outfits. Apparently the feature is going to run the same
week as the big-band week. We all looked very suave and
sophisticated! It was a very funny morning and we had a
right old laugh. Then it was off to rehearsals in the afternoon – busy busy busy.

SATURDAY, 12 JANUARY 2002

Arrived at the studio about 9am. It's Nicki Chapman's turn to be away this week so the boys were misbehaving. Simon, Foxy and Pete were throwing a right old strop today – arguing between themselves over why they chose Abba as the theme. By the time they got to me they just went off on one at me. How dare they do that before I'm about to perform? Talk about putting you off your stride. Although it wasn't directed at me I have to say it knocked my confidence for six.

Decided on a cream jacket and my dad's brown suede flares which he bought to win my mum over when they were courting over 30 years ago – how cool is that? I had to text my dad to tell him that they were getting their first outing on national television. Underneath the jacket I wore, and you're going to laugh at this, Toni the stylist's green vest. We were searching for a top to go underneath the jacket but we couldn't find the right colour, then she produced this dark green vest and I had to laugh because when I put it on it came halfway up my stomach.

Spookily, when I went on stage and sung 'The Name Of The Game', I really wasn't concentrating – I could have been standing there wondering what to have for my tea! I was actually thinking about the judges in the dress rehearsal and I think it affected my performance. The judges weren't convinced by it, either.

Pete: 'It's a difficult one tonight. I don't want to be sitting here tonight, Will, because I thought you, all the way, pulled it off. I think it's tight tonight.'

Foxy: 'You know I think you're excellent. I love the way you sing. I think you're class, I think you're a great enter-tainer, I think you did pull it off. What you always cleverly do is you kind of start your song quite normal, then you kick in with a bit of Will in the second half. Anyone at home will agree you have the most expressive and move-able eyebrows!'

Simon: 'I admire you for making the song your own tonight, but I will say to you, like I've said to everyone this evening, that we are trying to create in this competition a pop idol to compare with the very best out there. Everything I've seen tonight has disappointed me so far. I think every-one is going to have to work very hard next week.'

Well, what do you say to that? I think I got off quite lightly compared to what they said to some of the others. Poor old Rosie was ripped to shreds, but this week was a difficult one for us all. None of us had a good show with the exception of Gareth. His performance of 'One Of Us' was incredible.

The interview with Kate Thornton wasn't brilliant either cos we were on such a downer, but she really is good at her job. To keep all of us lot under control, conduct a live interview and keep the pace is a lot harder than everybody thinks. I've got a lot of time for Kate.

And so it was time for the results. The judges were unanimous that Rosie would go and unfortunately the voters agreed and off she went. But I think she'd say that being on the Couch of Cruelty three times was quite enough. I know I wouldn't cope very well at all with that and so far I've been very lucky. I was really sad to see her go.

SUNDAY, 13 JANUARY 2002

Managed to sneak home for a couple of days of normality, which keeps my feet on the ground. My family wouldn't let me get big-headed anyway – we're just not like that. *Pop Idol*-wise we have started appearing more and more in the papers– it's best not to read them because even though I know what's going on in the competition it's still hard not to believe what the papers say even though some of it does stretch the truth. There's a feeling that they are really trying to build up the hype between the remaining five of us – thank God we all get on!

MONDAY, 14 JANUARY 2002

Decided to drive to Exeter and see some of my old uni friends. Tried to learn the words for my big-band tune on the way. I keep wondering if I should have changed this song for a Sinatra number but I don't want to fall into the trap of performing it like Sinatra – you can't replicate a genius. I think it will be better to keep this Harry Connick Jr tune because it's new to me and it's better to make a song I've only heard a few times my own rather than attempt a classic that could never be made my own. Ever!

Eventually arrived and met up with a few uni friends, then went to a gorgeous pub on the river in Exeter. It was so nice to go back and visit a place that I have so many fond memories of.

TUESDAY, 15 JANUARY 2002

Went and had lunch in Harry's restaurant – it felt like I'd never been away. I'm sure if I'd got behind the bar I'd have remembered everything – God, I sound like I've been away for years when scarily it's only been four, maybe five, months since I left! Drove back and am now really tired.

WEDNESDAY, 16 JANUARY 2002

Up early this morning because we had to go and do a photo shoot with *Smash Hits* magazine which I find hilarious and weird both at the same time, because everyone always used to read it when we were younger and now I might be in it! Then this afternoon we went to Chiswick to the Power Station studios (or something like that) and we rehearsed with the Big Blue band. I WAS SO EXCITED! Walked into the rehearsal room and the band sounded so loud, but once I'd had a practice the volume seemed completely normal. These songs we're doing are great. I'm looking to play it straight and then I'll sort out changes and stuff with David and Carrie tomorrow. Singing with a band is something I've wanted to do for so long – and there I was doing it. Absolutely amazing. Oh my God, can you believe we're going to a film premiere tomorrow? How funny is that? It's for a new action film called *Black Hawk Down* and we're really excited. But what are we going to wear?!

THURSDAY, 17 JANUARY 2002

Today was hilarious – we had lots of press to do. I for one was up early and in my car doing a radio interview on the phone – who said that showbiz was supposed to be glamorous? Then at lunchtime I had my vocal training with Carrie and David but Gareth, Zoe, Hayley, Darius and I were getting very excited about the evening ahead – the film premiere! So it was back to the hotel and there was lots of filming going on of us getting ready. Can't believe they filmed me in my towel – cheeky sods!

I wore a black suit with a white shirt underneath. Darius was all in black and looked so much classier, but then he is the Mr Smooth of the group. Gareth went for the grey metallic suit, black shirt and silver tie and the ladies were both looking glitzy in their respective shimmery outfits. When I saw what the others looked like (and they did look amazing!) I started to panic – mainly about tripping up on the red carpet! Off we toddled to our limo (which, by the way, we had to get in three times because we were being filmed) and eventually set off for Leicester Square. Spoke to Foxy on the way, which was all very bizarre because we were speaking to him as a DJ and not one of the judges, and then we were there. There were so many people there. I was the first out of the car – flash, flash, flash, flash – so many photographers and TV crews. I could hear this one person just screaming my name really loudly, which made me feel really good… for about five seconds, because as the others got out of the car one by one she did the same for them. Talk about fickle fans! On the way in we posed for group photos and Hayley and Zoe got to have their picture taken with Josh Hartnett. Then we were all off talking to the TV crews. Someone asked me if I was wearing anything designer, to which I (wittily, I thought!) replied, 'Yes – M&S boxer shorts!' Is that funny? The film was good but it did make me feel really sick – there was this one scene when they had to put someone's hand into a wound and up into the heart. And I obviously wasn't alone because some poor person passed out behind me! It was a great film though. Then we went to the premiere party – amazing place, amazingly done up, amazing canapés, but a very strange experience. People came up and quoted their job titles at me – 'Hiiiiiii, I'm blah from blah' – and I just thought, that's nice, all we could say was, 'We're singers.' It was a great experience but it was good to get back to the hotel with just us lot and sit and have a laugh together. Normally I love meeting new people but this evening was very strange. Why do the same celebrities turn up to these things every time? It can't be that exciting. Surely they must get bored? I'm not being ungrateful because the whole evening was a real treat, but I wouldn't make it a thing that I do if I was famous. If I had a night off I'd probably choose to go for a meal with friends because it'd be more fun.

FRIDAY, 18 JANUARY 2002

Oh my God, we're all over the papers today! I can't believe I look such a mess compared to the others – why didn't somebody tell me?! I suppose I've only got myself to blame! Had loads more press to do today – a photo shoot for a new magazine (so new I don't even know the title of it!) and then it was on to rehearsals. It was a long one today and Zoe cried, not because she was tired and emotional but because she was so happy to be singing with this amazing band – and although I was shattered I knew exactly how she felt!

SATURDAY, 19 JANUARY 2002

Arrived early as usual and we had all the normal rehearsals today. Getting ready for the dress rehearsal was great and emotional all at the same time. I chose a suit with a black tie and white shirt, and with that I wore my grandfather's cufflinks and watch from the 1930s – very fitting for the big-band show. I can't believe he's been gone a year – I still really miss you, Bobby! He has been an amazing inspiration to me for this competition – especially for the big-band songs because he actually saw the Glenn Miller Band when he was in the RAF. It really geared me up to do well – I knew he'd be watching over me.

So we were down to five – Hayley, Darius, Gareth, Zoe and me – and we knew (don't ask me how!) we were going to have such a great time. What an amazing show – I loved performing 'We Are In Love'. I think the audience were waiting for Will to sing Frank Sinatra and instead they got Will singing a great jazz song that probably most of them hadn't heard of. But tonight I did it for Bobby.

Zoe sang 'Get Happy', Hayley sang 'That Old Devil Called Love', Gareth performed 'Mack The Knife', then it was me and then Darius finished the show with 'Let's Face The Music And Dance'. We were all bloody brilliant (even if I do say so myself) but Gareth's 'Mack The Knife' was incredible – I really do think he could be the winner. Absolutely awesome. And Zoe was mind-blowing – how could you fail to smile after a performance like that? Actually, tonight was the first time I watched everyone else's performances and I was suitably impressed!

Pete: 'Right, Will, first let's start with the negative, OK? It may be Ant's favourite song but he's a TV presenter so what does he know? Actually, you did a brilliant job on what I think is a lousy song. I think the band were brilliant and you were staggering because I think if you'd had a good song you would have been overpowering tonight. I think you are brilliant. I think you made that song yours but that song is nowhere as good as you. I wouldn't have picked that.'

Simon: 'He does go on, Pete, doesn't he? Take no notice. I thought you were brilliant, the band were great, the song was great. Nicki?'

Nicki: 'Praise indeed. You were born to sing with yes, a big voice, a big band – perfectly suited. But the one thing with you, Will, is you could be a swinger from any era – you sit perfectly. Well done.'

Foxy: 'Well, you are definitely the jam in my doughnut. You are a Ferrari Testarossa more than a pair of socks in a

Christmas present. You were brilliant – I have always admired the way you sing particularly in the last ten. A brilliant performance.'

All the judges predicted Hayley would be next to go. No, not my Hayley Bayley – I've really bonded with her in this competition. Unfortunately the judges have become psychic and Hayley was voted out by the public – can't believe she's gone (who will I gossip with now?), especially when she was at her best tonight. She couldn't have done any better because her performance was sheer brilliance. But by now we've all realised that you're just going because someone has to go that week, not because it was a bad performance. She may have been out and there may have been a few tears shed backstage but even Hayley couldn't let the evening pass without going out for the birthday party of the century – there were twenty friends and family out to celebrate mine and Rupert's 23rd birthday. There were about five of us on the show celebrating birthdays so we made it a joint bash and off we went. Had a car race to Soho House which was v. funny – even Mum and Dad came and had a great time, with Dad announcing to the world, 'I'm so happy, I'm having so much fun!' Hmmm, either he was high on a good time or he'd had one too many lagers methinks! We stayed there until about 3am and the only bad thing was that on the way out the paparazzi had found out where we were and as soon as we walked out the door the flashes went. And just walking out that door people managed to have things nicked out of their bags and pockets. Rupert had his wallet and his phone taken and Claire the producer lost her camera. Shame it tainted such a great night. But I had to wait behind the door – I was all ready to walk out but everybody around me told me to wait until the cars were outside. It was a perfect example of people hyping up a situation when they really don't need to. The photographers were going to get their picture one way or another but everybody was drunk so it got a bit more dramatic than it should have. I got rushed out and it suddenly became this big thing. Anyway, after all the drama I came back to the hotel with Adam. It was so nice to catch up, but we had one of those stupid play fights – he pushed me, I pushed him back and this continued with both of us in hysterics. It resulted in me getting a massive cut on my head! The bloody sod – I'm gonna get him for this! We've got loads of press this week too – I hope the make-up will cover up the cut!

SUNDAY, 20 JANUARY 2002

It's my birthday today – yay! But that doesn't mean that the work stops! Today me, Zoe, Gareth and Darius had a press briefing (all in advance of a major press conference that's happening this week). It was just what we needed because now there's this huge press interest in us and it was great to understand and how it all works because we haven't done this before. Then it was off to Ray for the routining of the Number One songs for the next show. Have gone for 'There Must Be An Angel' by the Eurythmics and 'Night Fever' by the Bee Gees – don't think anybody will be expecting that one! The themes have been great so far, with the exception of Abba – one week we'd all like to put behind us! Ray Monk went through both songs with me and I actually had a lot of input with them, too, which is cool. So I have decided to just go for it and completely change both of the songs – David and Carrie aren't gonna know what's hit them!

MONDAY, 21 JANUARY 2002

Had photo shoot for a newspaper today. It's very strange doing all these sessions for the press – I still don't know what to do with my hands, or what face I'm supposed to be pulling. I think I just smiled to cover any worrying moments!

TUESDAY, 22 JANUARY 2002

We had the press conference today – how tense? I was really worried about what they were going to ask us. I started cracking a few gags – and I told the UK press that I wanted to have tea with the Queen when they asked me what my dream date would be. There's nothing worse than thinking you're funny, especially at a press conference, and I thought I was hilarious – I wasn't, but that didn't stop me thinking it! I was worried in case somebody asked about my sexuality becasue at this point in time I wasn't comfortable to talk about it.

Then it was off to do a photo shoot for yet another newspaper – today we were dressing up as our favourite pop idol. I've plumped for Jamiroquai. He is so amazing – what a funkster! It was hilarious prancing around the studios dressed as Jay Kay – you should have seen the headdress! I really got into the character! We didn't get back from that till late and we were all so tired, but the TV crew still wanted to film Darius cooking the dinner. Poor Darius was knackered as well but they even needed to film him doing the shopping – take after take. I think they're trying to make out that he does all the cooking – not true I might add, we've all been taking turns in the kitchen! Filming is such a nightmare – can't believe we couldn't even have dinner in peace. It was an extremely long day today and I'm just glad it's over.

THURSDAY, 24 JANUARY 2002

Did a shoot with *TV Quick* this morning and then had to go
through the Number One songs with David and Carrie –
I'm pleased with mine and they both seemed really positive.
It should be a fun show – such varied songs between the
four of us:

> Gareth is singing 'Wake Me Up Before You Go-Go'
>   and 'Unchained Melody'
> Darius is shaking his hips to 'It's Not Unusual'
>   and 'Whole Again'
> Zoe has picked 'I Wanna Dance With Somebody'
>   and 'The Power Of Love'

It's gonna be another toughie!

SATURDAY, 26 JANUARY 2002

Arrived at the television studios this morning but wasn't feeling my usual sparky self. I think it's just hit me that we're down to four people... out of 10,000! Unbelievable! It feels like the others have disappeared on holiday and will be back next week. I have become much quieter in the last couple of shows but I think it's because I'm finding the challenge a bit too much – most unlike me! We went through the usual processes (make-up, wardrobe, dress rehearsals) and I decided to wear a very cool outfit for this show – a black leather jacket with white stripes, pinstripe trousers and a pair of funky white shoes.

Then it was time for the show. Gareth was on first, followed by Darius then Zoe and last but not least, me. Their performances were brilliant – a little too brilliant for my liking! Performed 'There Must Be An Angel' and I thought it went well. Had to wait for the judges' comments until I'd sung my next song, 'Night Fever', which really got the crowd going. They were up on their feet and I felt on top of the world! Until the judges spoke, that is...

Foxy: 'Excellent as always – you start with your trademark head on a slant all doey eyed. Then you kick into Will and you make the song your own – that's what is always good about you. The reason you're becoming famous is because you've got a great voice.'

Simon: 'Will, very good! Frankly I think we have to judge everyone on their performance each night and I think I was talking to Pete, who brought it up – if I hadn't met you before and you were against Darius tonight I think Darius pipped you.'

That was followed by hilarious pantomime-style booing from the audience – ah well, at least *they* like me! But that wasn't all...

Pete: 'The great thing about this show, Will, is you've got some credits in the bank, because I actually agree with Simon. I think the last couple of weeks you ain't given us your best shot, son.'

More hilarious boos from the audience – at that point it really didn't look like the judges liked me. Even Nicki Chapman...

Nicki: 'You have great dexterity and power to your voice although I think the first track was a little more Dave Stewart than Annie Lennox, but you pulled it back on the second song and it was more Will for me.'

I just stood there, smiled sweetly and walked over to Ant

and Dec – and though that journey from the judges' spot to the presenters takes two seconds, it felt like an eternity. I felt completely dejected because 'There Must Be An Angel' had been the song that I'd had the most amount of input with. I was really upset with the slating I got for it. Maybe I hadn't given it my best shot or maybe I was just completely overre-acting? After all, it's the first time I've had any negative comments so maybe I was just letting it all get to me too much. I was thinking, If I get through this week I'm going to have to work my nuts off if I want a place in that final. And God, *DO* I really want it? It really hit me just how much I did want it when I thought I could be close to losing it.

At least Ant and Dec stuck up for me.

'The audience didn't agree, Simon. The audience thought you were talking absolute boll…derdash!'

I couldn't have agreed more!

Feeling a bit down, we went on to do our ITV2 interview with Kate… Can you believe I cried on national television? Of all the places! I'd had enough and I had this hideous feel-ing that I was going to go, and truthfully I was ready to go. God, I can't keep up with my moods! But I'd had enough of going through this week after week – it really is hard! After I'd dried the tears I had a bit of time to think over the judges' comments and, to some extent, I think Pete was right. I had gone off the boil a bit, particularly after 'Ain't No Sunshine' because if you think about it, it really was a massive performance and I have been struggling really hard to get that intensity back. I suppose once people have seen that you're capable of that sort of passion, that's what they're going to expect from future performances.

Tonight it's given me a glimpse into how vulnerable you are as an artist because I had a say in both those songs and I wanted them both, particularly 'There Must Be An Angel', to work. None of the judges liked it and I suppose they know what they're talking about, but I was gutted.

Before we knew it we were back out on stage, awaiting the results. I knew that if they said my name I'd be ready to leave...

Did the judges think I should go?

Foxy – Zoe
Nicki – Zoe
Pete – Zoe
Simon – Zoe

I couldn't believe they had all chosen Zoe. I really thought this was going to be my week to be the judges' choice to leave. Then Ant and Dec read out the results... My heart was pounding – it was Zoe! Oh my God, I'd made it through to the final three, but I was so upset to be losing Zoe. We'd all become good friends and now we'd lost the only girl. Gareth was in floods of tears – he'd lost his best friend in the competition and was inconsolable. She's a wonderful girl with a remarkable talent and so mature for her age. I hope we'll be seeing a lot more of Ms Zoe Birkett.

After the show we had another interview with ITV2 – I don't think we've ever been so downhearted. But we didn't have much time to mope because as soon as we had finished the interview, Darius and a tear-stained Gareth and I had to have a meeting with Simon Cowell. He played us two songs (both of which didn't do much for me but to be honest I really wasn't in the mood to be appreciating music) and told us that as of tomorrow, the three of us would be going into a studio to record what will become the winner's first single. And whilst part of me thought, Bloody hell, that could be me, another part of me thought, Who cares? I have never been on such an emotional rollercoaster.

SUNDAY, 27 JANUARY 2002

Well, you can't say they hang around in this competition because today was one of the most exciting for me. We were recording what could be my debut single! BLOODY HELL! One of the songs we're laying down, 'Evergreen', is a track from a Westlife album, written by hit makers Jörgen Elofsson, Per Magnusson and David Kreuger. The other is a song written by Cathy Dennis – she wrote Kylie's 'Can't Get You Out Of My Head' – how cool is that? So we arrived at Olympic Studios in southwest London and met the producers of both songs and had run-throughs – I have to say on first impressions I wasn't over-struck on either of them. It almost felt like the songs had been chosen especially for Gareth – they were both great pop music but written in a style more suited to his voice. I'd be lying if I said I don't think the winner has already been decided, and the papers seem to be hyping that too. I found 'Evergreen' a very difficult song to get into – I wasn't motivated and I find it very hard to sing songs if I'm feeling like that.

Anyway, I went into the studio to record 'Evergreen' and I was up front and told the producers I was having a bad day and was really tired, and that I was struggling with the song – well, I thought it best to be honest so I didn't leave the studio with them thinking I was being arsey. They just told me to go with the flow and do whatever I needed to do to make it mine. That was all I needed to hear to give me a little boost. I told them I just needed a way in and that when I got there it would be good. So after working hard on it, I think I've cracked it. I hope the producers respected my honesty about the song. The fact that they just told me to do whatever I wanted made me respect them even more.

And I know I got there because, as Nicki Chapman would say, I made the song my own! It was a difficult one but I think I managed it.

MONDAY, 28 JANUARY 2002

I was back at the studios today to record 'Anything Is Possible' with Cathy Dennis. She seems nice and knows exactly what she wants from a record. We worked hard together on this song because like 'Evergreen' it was another song that I found difficult to work with. But after speaking to Cathy and trying to make the song belong to me, I think we did it! Although I have moaned I have completely enjoyed myself the last couple of days. I've always wanted to record a single and even if mine is never released, it's still an experience I will cherish. And it's made me even more determined to have a career as a singer.

TUESDAY, 29 JANUARY 2002

I had so much to do today – first we had to return to the studios to finish bits and bobs on both singles. It's very strange because whilst one of us has been with one producer another has been recording with the other one and the third person has been busy working closely with one of our press officers from Pearson, filling in questionnaires for newspapers and magazines. Confusing but all great fun. Plus we were being interviewed by *Popworld* magazine and having to record mini interviews for radio stations around the country! Not much then! To top it all, we then had to go back to the hotel and pack because tomorrow we're supporting S Club 7! (I can't believe I forgot to write that in!) We were worried on Saturday night that we might be going to Dublin to perform at a concert and then they told us that we would be supporting S Club 7 on the first night of their tour. Hang on, let me write that again – we're supporting S Club 7 on the first night of their tour! OH GOD!

WEDNESDAY, 30 JANUARY 2002

Flew to Dublin and went straight to the venue – it's MASSIVE! We also did a bit of filming on stage, which is where we met S Club 7 (what a lovely bunch of people they are), but then one of our cameramen, James, fell down one of the secret holes in the stage – camera and all! There had been a mix-up in communication with the production desk: they had opened the hole early for some reason and poor James fell backwards into it and broke his leg! After he had been rushed to hospital, we all had a run-through on the stage, which was absolutely amazing although very strange because there was no audience. We're going to be singing the last two songs that we sang on Saturday's show – 'There Must Be An Angel' and 'Night Fever' for me, 'It's Not Unusual' and 'Whole Again' for Darius and 'Wake Me Up Before You Go-Go' and 'Unchained Melody' for Gareth. S Club 7 were watching us rehearse, along with some of the crew, which was slightly unnerving. Then we watched them rehearse – they must have been a bit nervous, too, because it was their first night.

Then before we knew it, it was time to go on stage. Ant and Dec had both come over to Dublin to introduce the three of us – Darius went first and I was standing backstage watching him absolutely terrified! He was brilliant and you'd never know that this was his first time on stage in front of that many people – he was just riding the wave! And the crowd went wild as he thrust his hips to 'It's Not Unusual' – hilarious! As Darius came off Dec went on and introduced me to the audience... Words really cannot explain that feeling when you walk on stage! You are just hit by this huge wave of noise and you can't see anything except for lots of glo-sticks being waved from side to side. But there was an amazing response from the audience, which surprised me because they were only there for S Club 7 and we were just 3 guys in a competition. But they were great and I loved performing – I love working an audience. That's another thing that Arts Ed taught me – you have to take in the whole audience. You can't miss people out, in a theatre, in a concert and in life! I loved having the freedom of performing and not auditioning, but I half expected to see the judges rise up from the front of the stage! To have that space to perform on was incredible and that we didn't have to stand on a white Sellotape cross as we do in the studio was so nice. I can honestly say it is an experience that will stay with me for ever. I really didn't want to come off stage but I had to because it was the turn of Gareth. The screams were deafening!! He looked so nervous as we hugged each other before he went on. The crowd went completely hyper and he didn't disappoint – after the first song he had them all in the palm of his hand. He's going to win this competition – just one look at his performance and the reaction of this audience told me all I needed to know.

Then we joined Nicki Chapman and Simon Fuller in the audience to watch the S Club 7 show. I was so excited – my first pop concert, and I have to say S Club 7 didn't let me down. It may not be the type of music I would listen to normally but what a show! I was impressed by all of them – they have so much energy. The dancers were fantastic, too, but I think I noticed those more cos of all my dancing at Arts Ed! Afterwards we went back to the hotel where Ant and Dec were already in the bar – typical! But they did treat me to my first-ever pint of proper Irish Guinness and then we went out to the after-show party and just had a laugh with everyone. Everyone was, I'm afraid to say, a little worse for wear! If Ant and Dec ever offer you a drink I have three words of advice… turn them down!

To top it all, we have to fly back early tomorrow to do a photo shoot for the potential sleeve for the potential single. Things are hotting up!

THURSDAY, 31 JANUARY 2002

It was an amazing photo shoot today and considering how rough we looked and felt, I think we came out of it pretty well! I put on a Nicole Farhi suit, looked in the mirror and I was like, 'Wow, that can't be me.' But it was – amazing what a bit of slap and a good suit can do for you! Then this evening we had filming to do until about midnight – it was this hilarious sketch where we were all planning on killing each other off with the help of one of the others. Me and Gareth were plotting to cut Darius's head off. Well, he can't sing if he doesn't have a head – ha ha!

It has been a mad week I have recorded two potential singles, flown to Dublin, met and supported S Club 7, watched my very first concert (for someone who loves music so much, how shocking is that?), worn a Nicole Farhi suit (hello!) and had photos taken for the possible cover of my single… if I win!

Then it was back down to earth with a bump – vocal training with Carrie and David. It suddenly brought the

competition back to me because we'd gone from the freedom of performing on this massive stage in Dublin to real-
ising that one of us had to go on Saturday. I can't believe
how quickly we are down to three. This Saturday's theme is
the judges' choice – as if they don't have enough say in this
show! I have been busy working on 'Beyond The Sea'. I bet
Pete had something to do with that one! And 'Sweetest
Feeling' originally recorded by Jackie Wilson. Both
completely amazing songs and I've had a great time trying
to make them belong to me. I hadn't heard the Bobby Darin
one before so I've been learning that from scratch, and I love
'Sweetest Feeling' anyway – an extraordinary song. I just
hope they work their charm on Saturday though!

FRIDAY, 1 FEBRUARY 2002

I can't believe it's February already – this competition has just flown by. Rehearsals were in full swing today – there was a really nice atmosphere in the studios as well. We're all over the papers at the moment and (I promised myself I wouldn't look but I must admit I did sneak a peak) judging by their polls, it's not going in my favour! In fact, the *Sun* is saying that Gareth is going through for definite and that 'Darius pips Will' – well, that's just great, isn't it? Cut me down before I get a final chance to rest my case. It feels like it's over before we've even performed for this show – I know I'm going to have to pull something pretty special out of the hat tomorrow if I want a chance of going through!

SATURDAY, 2 FEBRUARY 2002

Woke up this morning feeling, well, I don't really know how to describe it but put it this way, it wasn't good! I was very nervous – possibly the most nervous I've ever been. Everybody around me was saying they'd never seen me this nervous. Got to the dress rehearsal and anyone that came near me could see that I was a bit wound up so they left me to myself!

The clothes were great – I've got two outfits to wear. Have decided that I'm going to wear a black jacket, a white T-shirt, black sparkly trousers and white shoes for 'Beyond The Sea' – another Toni spectacular! As for 'Sweetest Feeling', am going to go a bit more casual, with my black shirt, green baggy trousers and black-and-white trainers.

There was such a massive buzz in the audience tonight. In the first part of the show Darius was singing 'Dancing In The Moonlight' by Toploader, Gareth was singing 'Yesterday' by the Beatles and I was singing 'Beyond The Sea'. Could you get three more different songs? Darius was up first – he looked very suave (as only Darius can) but I don't think the song did his performance any justice. The audience went crazy but I thought he would be disappointed. Next up was Gareth – well, what can I say? Amazing as usual.

I really was bricking it when I walked on to that stage. I'd never admitted to myself before how much I wanted to get to that final – it scared me how much I wanted it. It all started off OK and I was really getting into the swing of things until disaster, I forgot my words about a third of the way through, and because of the way the backing track of the song runs there was nowhere to distinguish where exactly I was in the song. I just kept thinking over and over, Come on, Will, you can do this. This is the most important audition of your life and you've forgotten the words – oh yes, and now you've forgotten the place in the song. I couldn't believe it was happening and I really thought I wouldn't be able to finish the song. I've never really fluffed a performance but this sure looked the way it was heading. Then suddenly from nowhere (thank God!) it just popped into my head. It felt like a very spiritual moment because I just thought that someone somewhere must have been helping me out because for a moment I promise you there wasn't a cat's chance in hell that I was getting back into that song!

Then it was time for the judges' first comments…

Pete: 'Earlier in the series, right about Christmas, I pointed out that Will had a resemblance to Bobby Darin.

Great voice, Frank Sinatra-ish, and this is a Frank song that Bobby went on to make his own. Although I learnt it at school in 1954, I just thought I would love to hear it. We all thought that this was a cracking song for you to sing. It's one of my favourites too.'

See, I knew Pete had something to do with it. My other song was 'Sweetest Feeling' by Jackie Wilson and I came out on to that stage thinking that I didn't care about anything – not because I didn't care but because I just thought if I can pull off an amazing rescue like I did on 'Beyond The Sea' then I CAN DO ANYTHING! So I really went for 'Sweetest Feeling' – I don't think I've ever had such control over a song and that's testimony to David and Carrie and how far we've all come as singers, especially after Darius belted out 'Make It Easy On Yourself' (originally I think by The Walker Brothers) and then Gareth got 'em going with 'Flying Without Wings'.

Were the judges going to be harsh? It was time to find out…

Simon: 'It feels so weird to be nice the whole time! It's unusual, but a fantastic, strange feeling.'

Nicki: 'I think you gave us all the sweetest feeling, that was absolutely fantastic. For me, the measure of a true artist is when you can do something for everybody, and when you performed "Beyond The Sea" I think from fifteen-year-old girls to 65-year-old music lovers, they would have all adored that version. You were absolutely tremendous, a fantastic performer for everybody. Well done!'

Crikey, so far so good!

Pete: 'Will, here we go, son, are you ready for this? I have given you stick over the past three weeks because I think you've picked the wrong songs. See what happens when you sing the blinkin' great songs, you are blinkin' great! Fantastic, that was as good as Jackie Wilson. Everybody north of Watford will be sitting and bouncing around their kitchens to that one. Fantastic.'

Excellent!

Foxy: 'Do you know, Will, brilliant! You know I love your voice. Your effortless style is good. But do you know, the people in the music business have been giving us a hard time about this programme, saying it's not the way you should be finding talent, and I would like to say, as we sit here in front of thirteen, fourteen million people that we have three great singers, three amazing songs, well, six amazing songs tonight. THIS is what it's all about, it's fantastic. Well done!'

All that extra work was worth it. I just hoped the public agreed! Even Ant and Dec were impressed...

Dec: 'Man, you busted tonight! You ripped it up.'

Ant: 'Well done. Calm down, Dec!'

Dec: 'Got a bit overtaken there, but they really suited you, both songs.'

'It's been great actually,' I said, 'and I did agree with Pete. I think I had made some mistakes over the past weeks and perhaps got a bit sort of "Ah, I can do this," but these songs

I sang tonight were fantastic and they've really grown on me over the last week and it's been great to do a jazz song and then a Motown song.'

Ant: 'Because I think for you, if you go back to the weeks like when we did Abba, and you haven't really done them as well, probably because you don't really like those songs. Tonight, though, you loved those songs and look how well you've done them.'

To which I replied, 'I HATED Abba! I can say it now!'

Ant: 'Glad you're honest, mate!'

So am I! And I was keeping my fingers crossed – this was the first time I actually thought I was in with a chance!

Went off for what could have been my last chat with Kate and the ITV2 gang. I know we had a really good interview but my head is too fuzzy to remember what we spoke about. Then we were told that the final results were in and that we had to go back to the stage.

Who were the judges going to choose seeing as they had been so complimentary to all three of us?

Simon: Darius
Foxy: Darius
Nicki: Darius
Pete: Darius

Blimey, another clean sweep – I just kept my fingers crossed that for my sake the judges had got it right again! Sorry,

Darius! The three of us sat on that couch just waiting for the immortal words.

We had practised everything else in the dress rehearsal but the one thing we didn't know was how Ant and Dec were going to announce who had lost... They started with Darius, and normally the first person they went to would be the guaranteed safe person so of course I thought that was it immediately – I thought I was out. But they came to each of us... and just went over what we had sung. Talk about stringing it out! I was incredibly nervous. Then they told Gareth he was through and then they said, 'The second person in the final next week is... Will!' I stood there and thought, Oh my God, Oh my God – they just said my name. And for the first time in the competition I wasn't sad about losing someone and I wasn't sad for Darius because I knew he'd be alright. It was the first time I was completely happy for myself.

We had a great interview with Kate afterwards and Gareth really made me laugh – Kate asked him to sum up in three words how he was feeling and Gareth was stammering and then he just said to himself, 'Come on, it's only three words.' Which I thought was the best line of the whole evening. At the beginning of the competition I thought he was quiet and shy but he's not, and tonight made me realise how difficult it has been for him to get his true character across. He's got such a brilliant sense of humour and slowly but surely we are seeing a bit more of the real Gareth. This next week's going to be a laugh, and I know we won't be competitive.

Ant and Dec said afterwards that I was hyperventilating as they read out the results. I honestly don't remember that – all I can remember was being so damn nervous.

Then we had more meetings – this is starting to get serious. Simon Fuller and Nicki spoke to us about what was coming up in the next week but to be honest I still couldn't believe that I'd got so far so I wasn't paying a great deal of attention. I left the room to meet my family and friends who were waiting. They were so happy for me, and I have to admit I was happy for me, too!

SUNDAY, 3 FEBRUARY 2002

Talk about the morning after the night before. Urgh – had to be up early this morning (never a good thing in my book!) because this next week will revolve around a massive 'Vote For Us' campaign and Gareth and I had a press conference about it today. We will travel around canvassing for votes – at TV studios, radio stations – and meet the public wherever possible! They had us in suits, with rosettes (Gareth's was orange and mine was blue) – we looked like MPs running for Parliament. We both gave our manifestos (completely jokey, of course).

Gareth's was:

1. Not to throw celebrity strops or become a high-maintenance pop star.
2. To keep his hairstyle (the 2-2-1 formation).
3. Not to give photo shoots in exquisite mansions claiming them to be his home.

4. To work hard and give his fans everything they deserve for giving him this opportunity.
5. Not to become a celebrity big head.
6. Not to accept lavish gifts from other celebrities in a bid for publicity!

And mine was:

1. Not to throw celebrity strops.
2. To stay true to myself and my beliefs at all times.
3. Not to become a music-industry diva.
4. Not to request lychees on tap.
5. To shun celebrity hangouts.
6. To respect and entertain fans.
7. Not to wear trousers at an unacceptable waist height!

It was completely hilarious and we had a great laugh. Spotted a few of the Sunday papers and Gareth and I were all over them – I can't believe this can make front-page news. *Pop Idol* really has taken over the public's imagination!

Managed to have the afternoon off and meet Adam for lunch and do a bit of shopping. I'm really lucky that my friends have been so supportive because I don't think I could have got this far without them.

Tonight me, Gareth and Zoe (yes, she's still with us, bless her) came up with a great idea and made up this competition for our week of campaigning. We have to see

who can get something blue, something borrowed, the
best blag, the best autograph and the best freebie – should
be a laugh!

MONDAY, 4 FEBRUARY 2002

Up early today – 5.30am to be precise. We'd heard that we were getting our own buses to take us around but when we saw them, well, for once I was gobsmacked. It was this massive coach with blacked-out windows and huge pictures of me and my cheesy grin staring right back at me – very freaky, particularly at that hour of the day! But the highlight for me was the inside – it really did have everything you could need, apart from having to stare out from my receding hairline! Anyway, this campaign was hardcore work and today we had a 6.30am call time for *GMTV*. Mmm, nice! Met Eamonn Holmes and tried to nick his cereal bowl but felt guilty and put it back! Did that plus recorded a quick chat with Lorraine Kelly (and nicked a script from her show, which was blue, and got an autograph). Then it was back on the bus and I suddenly realised that I had an entourage with me – most strange. There was Faye my newly appointed PA, Cat from our press office, Henry's House, who would be looking after any press enquiries, Howler (Claire), one of the *Pop Idol* producers, Kim, Helen (who did hair and make-up and is so sweet) and four members of the TV crew. Plus there was my official photographer for the bus, too – mmm, not many people then! Next up were interviews with the *Daily Express*, *Daily Star* and *OK!* – turned up at the Express Building in Blackfriars and it was mad – so many people just waiting outside... to see me! I turned to Kim, one of the researchers on the show, and asked him how all these people knew I would be here. He just told me to turn around and then of course there's my bloody great big battle bus emblazoned with the hugest pictures of me I've ever seen and Vote Will written all over it – I suppose that might have been something to do with it! I did my interviews then got back on the bus to chat to *PA News* then it was off to Grosvenor House where I was about to conduct possibly the most television interviews I'll ever do in one day. Between 1pm and 5pm I hosted thirteen interviews – it's just as well I can talk for England, that's all I can say! Must admit to nicking one of the hotel's dressing gowns and a beautiful tea box – bet Gareth isn't doing as well!

Later on I went to Leicester Square to Capital Radio HQ – home to the one and only Neil Fox! Foxy had obviously been telling his listeners that Gareth and I would be visiting him and when I turned up I couldn't believe the number of people waiting outside – there must have been at least two maybe three hundred... We had no security so I'm amazed we got through. People were pulling my arm back and grabbing me – luckily Claire and Kim were helping me, and Leighton from the radio station waded in to lend a hand as well. Claire – the smallest of us all – was pushing her way through and ended up hurting her shoulder. Even worse, Leighton ripped his Prada shoes! Eventually we got into the swanky studios to see Foxy. I know we had already been interviewed by him when we went to that *Black Hawk Down* film premiere, but I still found it all very strange that I wasn't talking to him as a judge on the show. He was great – very funny – and made full use of the fact that me and Gareth are campaigning against each other. Well, that's what they all think but me and Gareth know that it's not like that at all. Managed to blag a gold disc of Anastacia's and a pig (not a real one). Decided to text Gareth to see how he was doing and it sounded like he was having as much fun as me. I arranged to meet him back at the hotel afterwards for a gossip and a large drink... of orange juice for him! Spoke to Pilky, who told me that she and Hugh had been sitting in a cafe in Leicester Square when they saw this massive bus drive past and my smile beaming down on them. Hilarious! I'm glad they saw it though because it's one of those things that needs to be seen to be believed! Am completely knackered and just need to crash. Never has my bed been more inviting.

TUESDAY, 5 FEBRUARY 2002

Not up quite as early as yesterday but we met about 8.30am and made our way through London to the South Bank where I was being interviewed on *This Morning*. The last time I was there was when the final ten had been announced and we all popped in for a chat, but this time it was just me and it felt really strange not to have everybody else around me. In the Green Room I spotted some of the newspapers and how funny is this? The papers have picked up on mine and Gareth's little competition – brilliant! Really enjoyed my interview with Fern Britton and John Leslie, who were both lovely and asked easy questions! I got a signed *This Morning* apron and a signed cushion from their sofa – might get this mini competition underway properly! Finished that and then met a journalist from *The Telegraph* who was coming with me on the bus to do an interview as I travelled to my next destination... Radio 2! On the way I sent a text message to my dad telling him I was on the bus to the BBC and he sent one back saying, 'Good boy – it's less expensive than a taxi!' Bless him – he has no idea what's going on in my life this week!

Got to Broadcasting House and met DJ Steve Wright. He's a nice bloke and we had a real laugh in the interview, plus I managed to get his watch for the competition! Wonder what else can I get my hands on?

On the way out I met some of my fans. It was so lovely to meet them – after all, if it wasn't for them I wouldn't be here! Some of the school kids asked me to sing something for them so I treated them to a dose of 'Night Fever' – it was such a laugh! But I found it really weird that people have to touch me. I don't know why that is – maybe it's like, Oh right, that's him. But a lot of the time it was pats on the back to say well done which was really nice. I wanted to say hello to everybody but we just didn't have the time so I kept apologising! Luckily Faye was there to play bad cop and whisk me away when I had to go.

Had interviews over at the *Sun* and the *News of the World* and then met a journalist from the *Guardian* who joined us on the battle bus. It's been great doing interviews as we're moving about from venue to venue because a. it passes the time and b. it's like a mini luxury office in the bus anyway! The only tedious thing is that I keep being asked the same questions again and again...

Yes, I am afraid.

Yes, my parents are proud.

Yes, I am happy.

Yes, I did always want to be a singer.

Yes I do REALLY get on with Gareth.

Anyway, finished that and made our way back to the BBC for an interview with Chris Moyles. I was a bit nervous because I've listened to him interview people before, but he was actually really lovely! On the way out I nicked their life-size Lara Croft – it was hilarious trying to run off with it! Unfortunately I had to give it back – spoilsports! Sent Gareth more text messages telling him we were beating him. Got out to the bus only to find the lovely Di knocking on the door of my bus, claiming that she was my friend to some of the bus crew who wouldn't let her in. We had parked outside her office and she said she just looked out of the window and saw me spread all over this bus. Brilliant – a friend to experience my fun! It was so nice to see her.

Then it was off for more interviews with the *Observer*, *The Times*, the *Independent* and the *Sunday Mirror* all on the bus – nice! Then it was back to the hotel for a catch-up with Gareth.

WEDNESDAY, 6 FEBRUARY 2002

Oh my God – had to get up at 5am today – 5AM!!!! We had a long old day recording radio appearances so it was off to Wise Buddah who had organised all these interviews around the country. I spoke to DJs from Scotland, Wales, Birmingham, and all over the south of England – basically a DJ in nearly every part of the UK from 7am till 10am. Managed to have a massive row with a DJ from Essex FM who clearly wasn't a fan of *Pop Idol* and I don't think we were ever going to see eye to eye, who asked me if *Pop Idol* was a cheap way of becoming famous. It really incensed me and I decided to turn the tables and ask him if he would enter a competition to find the best DJ. He wouldn't answer my question and I said, 'Well, I think I've made my point.' It just went from bad to worse after that – I had an answer for everything. He asked me if I'd had any bad experiences being on *Pop Idol* to which I replied, 'Only being on this show!' Well, I suppose I've had an easy ride so far – there had to be one bad apple! On went the professional smile and I carried on through the day. Had a couple more interviews to do in the battle bus on the way to places then ended the day meeting up with Gareth and recording a show with Graham Norton – it was brilliant but very strange because although we were in front of an audience neither of us were performing which, when you think about it, is all we've been used to for the last nine weeks! The audience went mental for us as we walked in. It was crazy! I suddenly realised how much people were talking about *Pop Idol* and how much it's become part of everyday conversation. Graham had been given the job of deciding who was to perform first on Saturday. I was heads and Gareth was tails. One flip of the coin and it was… heads! So I was going to be first – that will make a pleasant change! It has been a crazy few days but the excellent reaction from the media and the public has astounded me. Dare I say it? I think I could be in with a chance on Saturday.

THURSDAY, 7 FEBRUARY 2002

Back to normality – thank God. The last few days have just been crazy so it was really nice to go through my songs for Saturday with the lovely David and Carrie – although I did freak out because it was the last time I'd be with them. Actually, what am I going to fill my weeks with after this? One way or the other I will be leaving *Pop Idol* on Saturday and depending on what happens I could be going back to college next week! It will be ever so strange not to be routining on a Thursday with David and Carrie, rehearsing and getting styled on a Friday and then performing on the Saturday. My weekends are sure going to be empty from now on!

'Where did this lot come from?'

'It's just starting to sink in.' _ above
'I won!' _ top left
'That's more like it! Bring on the champagne!' _ bottom left

'Ant & Dec always made me laugh.'

'Four Wills for the price of one!'

'Hayley & I performing 'Ain't No Mountain High Enough'.'

'All I can say is thank you.'

FRIDAY, 8 FEBRUARY 2002

Had a very strange moment when we were doing the sing-throughs because Gareth and I were both watching each other perform – which doesn't sound too weird but we were singing exactly the same songs! Ant and Dec kept winding us up about how they're going to announce the winner. Went off to wardrobe with Toni, Tony and Nicole and for the 'Evergreen' performance I chose a great outfit. Black jumper (which I bought myself), a yellow and black belt, cords that are sort of black and gold at the bottom and yellow-and-black spider shoes.

Overall I feel really quite relaxed because I know I'll be leaving tomorrow in first or second place, which isn't bad! After the rehearsals we did a pre-record with ITV2 and I got into a heated discussion with the editor of *Heat* magazine over a feature they've run this week stating that my family didn't support and cheer for Gareth. Gareth and I were both very upset by the article. This show has been all about voicing opinions – we vented ours, the journalist voiced his and luckily we declared a truce at the end. The funny thing is, if anything, this actually brought our families closer together.

SATURDAY, 9 FEBRUARY 2002

The final! I couldn't quite believe the day was actually here when I woke up. I never dreamed I would get so far. Well, I may have dreamed it but I certainly never thought it would happen. Did a run-through of 'Evergreen' this morning but it didn't sound very good because my voice hadn't warmed up properly. I let out a massive scream of frustration because it was going so badly, which must have looked terrible because this was the first time I'd met the backing singers. They must have thought I was such a diva. I turned around and apologised to them: 'I'm so sorry. I just had to get that out of my system.' After that I was alright. It was very strange knowing that Gareth and me were going to be singing the same songs but luckily we had both managed to make our own marks on each song. We were both extremely anxious – I hadn't felt this bad all through the competition. Even Ant and Dec seemed nervous but then this was going to be one of the biggest shows they'd ever done, I suppose. I just assumed that because they're professionals they'd be

OK! Mum sneaked in backstage to see me before I went on and I have never seen her so excited.

The atmosphere was electric when me and Gareth walked out on stage and the crowd all had Will and Gareth flags which was hilarious. They were just going mental. I was actually feeling quite calm at this point. I had loads of people in the audience – Wiggy and Tim, Dominic, Jeremy, my grandmother, Mum, Dad, Rupert and his girlfriend, Emma and her boyfriend, Tom, Scottish Tom, Tall Andy, Adam, Katie, Diana, Stav, Hugh, Pilky, Milsy, Cally, Abby and Andy. Unfortunately James couldn't make it cos he's away – typical that my oldest friend is away in my hour of need! Not that he'd think I would have wanted him there, though – he'll laugh when he finds out that I, Mr Independent, wanted people around me! But it really was so good to have them all there. Oh nearly forgot – Fran was there too. She's just come back from India so had absolutely no idea what was going on. So for this to be her first 'Will on *Pop Idol* experience' freaked her out a bit I think!

Went offstage again and really had to concentrate on giving my best performance ever. I could tell it was going to be a tough night. I was first on and as I walked out the first thing that struck me was that the audience was much bigger than before – found out later they had put loads more chairs in to make extra room. There I was in my black jumper, yellow and black belt, cords and cool yellow and black spider shoes and I felt brilliant. Ant and Dec announced that

I was singing 'Evergreen' and off I went. I was really pleased with my performance and when I finished the crowd went mental. I just couldn't stop smiling! As I walked backstage I passed Gareth in the corridor and wished him luck – he was very nervous. Unfortunately I didn't get to see his performance because I was in the middle of my first change of the evening.

Then it was my turn again. This time I was performing 'Light My Fire' – this was my song and I wanted it to remind everybody why I was in this competition. Had changed into a black sleeveless top, my baggy olive-green trousers and my red and white trainers. There were massive screens all around me with flames everywhere and it went really well. Then I had to walk over to the judges – and no, I didn't trip this time! The audience were up on their feet and whooping and screaming – even Pete found it hard to get a word in edgeways!

Pete: 'I've used so many wonderful expletives about you but I saw one better tonight. Will, I'm British and I love you.'

I was so excited, all I could do was laugh…

Foxy: 'Will – fantastic. The nation has been gripped for four months by this programme. The last week's been nothing short of a frenzy and everyone's been expecting and looking forward to the big showdown. The both of you are being fantastic and I'm sure nobody has been disappointed by this but I'll tell you this for now, I want to buy your single, I will buy your album, I want to see you in concert and I will play your Number-One song!'

More laughing!

Nicki: 'Will, as you know I will be co-managing whoever wins tonight along with Simon Fuller, and both you and Gareth would be welcome additions to the 19 stable as well as all the superstars on the record company BMG. You are a multi-faceted performer tonight, you really are, and from vague auditions in the early stages to what I see in front of me tonight is a true superstar.'

Oh my God!!

Simon: 'Will, we're going to be working together so I'm going to be nice to you. I was wrong earlier on, I am happy to admit it. We're not always right in this business, but you totally deserve your place on here tonight. You are a super-star as they said – congratulations!'

I couldn't stop smiling and went off stage completely elated!

Then it was Gareth's turn to perform 'Flying Without Wings' – I really did think this would clinch it for him tonight. But I didn't have time to think about that – I had to get changed again for 'Anything Is Possible'. Changed into my pinstripe suit, coloured T-shirt and funky shoes. I was thinking, This is it, this is my last chance to shine. I went on, performed the song and really gave it my all. The audience went mad again, then Gareth came straight on after me to sing 'Evergreen' and I had to stand backstage and watch because I was on stage again as soon as he'd finished. I just walked on and gave him such a big hug – we were both great tonight but this was it – our future was now in the public's hands! And of course it wouldn't be complete without more chat from the judges...

Pete: 'You know what, I've had everybody say to me that the answer to the question is obvious – they know who's won and I say they don't know who's won. It is so close. Vote – you make the difference!'

Foxy: 'There were 10,000 people we saw trying to find the pop idol and we saw a lot of bad ones but tonight we found two very talented young men, let's be honest. I'm just happy to sit here and watch you become superstars and I'm just happy to sit here tonight to watch two great guys sing great songs. Well done!'

Nicki: 'You have both been sensational tonight, you really have, and what we know here is how strong your friendship is. This week you've been so loyal to each other and that is unique. Keep grounded. You both deserve the success.'

Simon: 'My last words – two winners, the most amazing production team, the best five months of my life and I want to thank ITV because without them this show wouldn't be on TV and I still think Pete Waterman is talking a load of you know what!'

The show finished with me, Gareth, Ant and Dec all clapping along with the audience. Then we just had to wait for the results! But we didn't have time to worry about that because it was straight into an interview with Kate on ITV2 and in between advert breaks we were being told that the lead kept swapping all the time – it was neck and neck! The adrenalin was kicking in and I just had to leave it in the hands of fate – if I was going to win then I was going to win. There were lots of good lucks as we walked back to the studio. I took a big deep breath and just thought, God this is it!

Gareth and I were sat on the couch as Ant and Dec told the viewers at home that the voting had smashed all records and that the lead had changed hands several times. Talk about give us butterflies… then they came and joined us.

Ant: 'You were both brilliant tonight. How do you feel now knowing the whole nation wants to know the result of *Pop Idol*?'

Gareth replied, 'My goodness, I'm so nervous.'

Ant: 'It's big, Will – it's massive!'

'I started hyperventilating,' I replied and then we all fell about laughing when we realised what Ant had just said.

Ant: 'I was talking about the voting! That's gone really well as well apparently. Everybody is talking about it. The nerves are kicking in and you're the two blokes left. It's phenomenal – did you ever think it would be as big as this?'

All I could do was shake my head and say 'Never' and poor old Gareth was just staring at the ground as though he'd gone off to another place.

Dec: 'Well, listen, whatever happens tonight both of you

have done fantastic and both of you are going to end up being massive stars. I think we've realised that!'

Then it was our chance to say thank you to Ant and Dec because they really had been fantastic to us all throughout the programme. Their humour and encouraging words really did mean a great deal to all the contestants.

Dec: 'It's been our pleasure to work with the pair of you and this has been a great TV experience for us that we're never going to forget either! So thank you all, too.'

Then we had a little montage of the series, during which I tried very hard not to cry – you know what I'm like! Plus a good luck message from Kylie Minogue – cool! Then there was a quick chat with the judges and a clip of me and Gareth singing 'Don't Let The Sun Go Down On Me' in the hotel earlier in the week.

And then...

Ant: 'This is it, the time is up. This is what the nation has been waiting for – we have the results.'

Oh my God, I thought, this is it!

Dec: 'Well done, guys, both of you – you've both done tremendously well to get this far. Out of 10,000 people you are the final two standing here! You've both performed brilliantly this evening and it's been very, very, very close. One of you got 4.6 million votes, the other one got 4.1 million votes – a total of 8.7 million votes is a new British record. So thank you all for voting. Whatever happens it's going to go in the *Guinness Book of Records* – it's the biggest TV vote

Britain has ever seen. But as you both know, guys, there can only be one pop idol. Best of luck to the pair of you.'

My head was pounding and my heart was racing. I was just thinking, Oh my God, oh my God. I stared into the audience. I couldn't see anything but I just kept staring straight ahead. Oh come on, let's just get on with it. And then it came:

Ant: 'OK, guys, the winner of *Pop Idol 2002* is... Will!'

Oh my God, this can't be right! What is happening? I just wanted to burst into tears – I clapped my hands to my face and stared around in disbelief. Everything happened in slow motion. I turned to Gareth and hugged him, then Dec and Ant, and I could see my family were going mental in the audience. I kept grabbing my stomach and then I heard Ant or Dec tell me to go and sing 'Evergreen' and I just flustered because I didn't realise what was happening. I thought, What do I do? Oh yes, just open my mouth and sing into the microphone! I started to sing and I dedicated it to Gareth. They had to put the words up on the stage because I kept forgetting them – luckily the floor manager Alan saw I was struggling. Then the confetti came pouring out of the studio ceiling and everybody came on behind me. I only thought it was the final ten and it wasn't until the end that I realised it was actually the final 50 – it was so nice to see so many familiar faces. I finished with a gob full of confetti and the next thing I knew Darius had picked me up and I was being carried on everybody's shoulders! It was like a big whirlwind because then I got carried off stage and went straight into a meeting with Simon Fuller and Nicki Chapman to discuss the videos, then on to ITV2 for the final interview with Kate – blimey, it was so hot in there I thought I was going to pass out. Then I was whisked off to the paparazzi for pictures. They were all shouting at me to look at them – I asked them to stop and said I'd work round all of them to make sure they got their picture. And it was after that that I eventually saw my family. They were blubbing with joy and I of course joined in! Eventually got to the bar where everybody was already partying, then later on came back to the hotel where my parents had hired a suite for us to party in (paid for with the £100 bet my dad put on me when the odds were 8/1 – how jammy is that?). Everybody was so happy, so drunk and so excited... but I have to fly to Cuba in five hours' time!

SUNDAY, 10 FEBRUARY, 2002

Not the best alarm call ever! I had to be up early today – or should that be I've only had a two-hour kip? Went to bed at 6am (whilst everybody else was still celebrating my win, I had to find some self-restraint and get a little bit of rest), got woken at 8am and was in a car with Faye and on the phone to *Popworld* magazine being interviewed at 8.30am while on the way to the airport to fly to Cuba, which is where I was making the videos for both of my singles. And just so I can remember this always, they are released on 25 February – my singles… MY SINGLES? Am I the only one who can't get their head round this? I just can't believe that I won – it really is too weird for words. I'm finding the transition from the show into the career incredibly difficult because that's what happened in the space of two hours. I felt extremely tired and very emotional – maybe I just need to rest. Had a massive fried breakfast at the airport then jumped on the plane at Heathrow and flew to Paris to get our connection to Cuba. Spent three hours hanging around in Paris airport which was actually fine because it meant I could try and get my head round (not advisable on two hours' sleep!) what was about to take over my life and go through my 'schedule' with Faye. My schedule, if you don't mind! Then we got on our connection to Cuba (flying club class!). I think I was being very annoying with my moving chair – I just kept pressing the button to move the back of the seat upright and all the way back again but hey, I've never flown club class before!

Arrived in Cuba and came straight to the hotel and it was strange. Here I am – I had spent the entire journey with Faye who is now my P.A. I've managed to get throught the last 22 years without one, with the exception of washing and allowance! She's a lovely lady and we've just started the 'getting to know you' process. I hope she doesn't find my independence too much; she seems as independent and honest as I am – we'll get there in the end.

MONDAY, 11 FEBRUARY 2002

This morning I was sitting in the lobby of a huge colonial-esque hotel in Havana. Even writing those words seems surreal and I think it sums up the whole *Pop Idol* experience for me. It has, without doubt, been the most strange, challenging, character-testing, exciting, extreme journey I've been on in my life. Something that started exactly five months ago has now finished and I'm the winner...WOW! I'm not sure when it will hit home. I always hoped I would do it. I don't know if that feeling is a quiet confidence and belief every performer should have, or if it was a deeper ingrained homing device, a kind of instinct of my pre-ordained success – I doubt it!

Anyway, here I am in Havana and first impressions are mixed. The first thing that's struck me is there doesn't seem to be a definite Cuban race – I mean, I know there is but it's not kind of pronounced. The thing I find myself asking is who comes to Cuba?

I called home today and found out there were lots of

journalists and cameramen surrounding my parents' house. That really upset me and made me feel incredibly guilty because I entered this competition, not my family, and now I'm thousands of miles away and I've left them at home to deal with all the frenzy. I never thought people would be interested in them and suddenly their home has been turned into a prison. Is this what it's going to be like? Maybe entering this competition was a mistake? I feel really alone and I can't relax and enjoy Havana for the beautiful place it is. I could tell everyone at home was as baffled by it as I was.

Faye and I sat in the cathedral square today – I just wish I could have chilled out a little bit more, because there I was sitting in this beautiful place drinking coffee with someone I hardly knew and it's hard work for both of us to get to know each other when we are shattered, stressed, in a different country and jet-lagged. I was really just feeling a bit homesick. We have discussed my schedule for the next three months, which is scary, but it was nice to know because I really needed to be on top of things so I can start to adjust to my new job. Next question – when's payday?!

TUESDAY, 12 FEBRUARY 2002

We went out to the countryside and climbed this beautiful hill – sounds boring but the scenery was amazing. I started to chill out and the view was incredible. We got to the top and there was a guy chopping coconuts. We drank the milk and on the way back we ate the coconut. Bonding over coconuts – bizarre but fun!

I asked if I could bring someone to Cuba with me and Milsy arrived this afternoon, which was just what I needed! I was glad she was there because I relaxed even more and had a good friend to talk with about my inner feelings. She came to the hotel and we stayed up until 3am chatting.

WEDNESDAY, 13 FEBRUARY 2002

Wandered around Havana and just chilled out with Milsy – bought some music and some pressies. You know, the usual touristy things. Had lunch in this wonderful square – there were bands playing everywhere. In fact, we sat down for lunch and suddenly noticed that we were sitting right opposite the microphones, the maracas and the bongos and Milsy even said she didn't think we were sitting in a good spot for a natter. Sure enough on came the band... RIGHT IN FRONT OF US! We couldn't move because it would have been too rude so we pissed ourselves laughing instead and decided to appreciate the music... Just chilled for the rest of the day and let the jet lag sort itself out.

THURSDAY, 14 FEBRUARY 2002

Valentine's Day and I'm miles away from home – I think I would have gone bananas without Milsy! Up at 5am to film the video for 'Anything Is Possible' – Greg the director is brilliant and we had a laugh which was really important. Sally the producer is lovely, as are Jo the stylist and Louise the make-up artist. Greg told me they're keeping both videos very simple – simple but stylish! Anyway the location people, Pete and Fiona, had done themselves proud and found these amazing ruins and a deserted park type place – it really reminded me of *Jurassic Park* actually. I kept expecting to see a pterodactyl swoop down from somewhere! And by the way, we might be in Cuba but the rain still came! Typical – miles from England and it still pours down – hope it looks good in the video! Anyway we finished about 9pm and I was knackered but I have had a great idea for a film! Cuba is a very inspirational place.

FRIDAY, 15 FEBRUARY 2002

Started at about 9am. The video for 'Evergreen' was being filmed in the most beautiful theatre today. It was roasting hot inside though and there was a lot of waiting around so I tried to hang out in my dressing room as much as I could because the doors opened up on to the streets of Havana and it was just so chilling to watch everybody going around doing their own thing. It's hard work not doing much! I'm very aware that I am the smallest part of this equation – all I have to do is turn up and sing. I didn't realise that so much prep goes into these video shoots – it's unreal. The Cuban people were wonderful though – especially those who made up my audience for the video. They paid me wonderful compliments but I still can't get my head round being a pop star! Finished at about 3am – knackered – night night!

SATURDAY, 16 FEBRUARY 2002

Did the beach shots for 'Anything Is Possible' and there are some great ones of me... when I was asleep. So if you think I'm being a bloody good actor I'm not – I really am asleep. I think the jet lag caught up with me. Glad Milsy was there though – she was amazing to have around. They should be good for a laugh when we get back home!

SUNDAY, 17 FEBRUARY 2002

Found out this morning that my flight back to the UK has been cancelled – well, it's a bit of a problem because I need to be back to record the *Pop Idol Winner's* show. It's a *Pop Idol* special where I perform along with a few of the final ten so really I need to get back to London pronto. Luckily the airline eventually found me a flight and I travelled back first class. The air hostesses had a nightmare with the food on the plane because we had really bad turbulence and they couldn't serve it, so I gave up waiting and just made my chair into a bed – very cool – and slept all the way home. Stopped in France and then reboarded on the UK flight only to see my mug sprawled over the front of the *Financial Times* – well, welcome back, Will. I'm really looking forward to this *Pop Idol Winner's* show because I'm going to be singing a duet with Hayley. 'Ain't No Mountain High Enough' has been chosen by the show and I'm really looking forward to performing with her, not to mention seeing her again. It has been another week on the *Pop Idol* crash course on how to be a singer/star – Week 11: Making the video! It's been the most mentally stressful week, having to get my head round winning the competition – I still get butterflies when I think about it. I sometimes just think, Oh no, what have you done? My life will never be the same! But I suppose it's better simply to go with the instinct that took you to that place – the thing that said inside of you, 'This is right for me!' At the end of the day, though, it's my family I'm worried about. For me it's a chance to take on another of life's challenges. This is what I've always wanted to do and now I'm doing it. I know there are going to be bad times but I've got the guts and courage to deal with them when they arrive – I hope! I'm sure my family will rise to the occasion, too – I've seen them do that before.

Got back home to the flat and there was nobody around – Mary wasn't there and – much worse! – there was no food in the house! So I put Billie Holiday on, sat down, lit a fag and called my mum. Then Mary came home (it was so nice to see her) and we phoned out for pizzas.

MONDAY, 18 FEBRUARY 2002

Up at 9am to get to rehearsals for the *Pop Idol Winner's* show and I was really looking forward to it… except since getting back from Cuba I've been suffering from diarrhoea – not nice! I had to learn all my new songs for the show because I hadn't had time out in Cuba. It's the words that worry me rather than the actual songs because my memory is horrific at the moment. Did enjoy it though despite being ill, it was lovely to see all the others (all of the final ten). I had to do an interview with Kate, which is being shown on ITV2 on Saturday and it was just as well it was pre-recorded because we had to keep stopping every five minutes so I could run to the toilet! You know what I thought about today? The fact that from the beginning of the final ten, we never argued, which in a group of ten strangers was amazing. Everyone was good at dealing with each other. I used to take myself away and people recognised that in me quite quickly. When people are having a moment you just leave them to it. don't you?

Even though I've only been away a week, it was a relief to see everyone again – it made me put things in perspective and remember what a good time we had. I really do think they're all incredibly talented people. Well, they must be – getting down to the final ten out of 10,000 ain't bad, is it? I'm going to write a bit about them all now in case I ever forget!

Korben – I admired his tenacity, drive and confidence and I really did think he had what it took to go all the way.

Jess – just gorgeous. I don't have a bad word to say about Jess. She's very funny and speaks very plainly and I admire that. She's never malicious, so when she says something people listen to her, which I think is an amazing quality to have. She and Rosie are like sisters – honestly, they go on at each other and wind each other up. They love each other to pieces.

Rosie has changed the most out of all the ten, for the better. She is very sensitive and thinks a lot, but knows herself very well and I think that's a very important thing. If you know yourself and how you work, then you can deal with things. I think she has come out on top to be honest. She's chilled out a bit; she just has a laugh. She makes me laugh because she goes through little mad patches and we all say, 'Oh God, Rosie and her five minutes of weirdness!'

Laura is bubbly, bubbly, bubbly, bubbly! She says all these things to me and I don't understand a word of them. I just nod and agree! I've got used to it now though. She's very sexy on stage as well.

Aaron is the joker, the Bernard Manning of the ten. He can't resist any sneaky little pun or anecdote or anything. He's a brilliant, brilliant guy.

Hayley is gorgeous – lovely, lovely Hayley. She has an amazing voice, and she's very bubbly, very kind, very thoughtful and just very normal, which is just what you need really. And now, luckily for me, a great, great friend.

Zoe is gorgeous too – only sixteen, and she's got all that going for her. You can hear her maturity in her voice, which is amazing, but it's her overall attitude that wins it for her. She has words of advice that took me a long time to get and I think that comes from her parents. She's brilliant.

Darius is probably the most complicated out of the ten. I can't help but admire his drive but I also can't help but find that a bit daunting. The good thing is that he doesn't blab about it though. Hayley was the same, she was in *Popstars* too, and I have massive respect for them both.

Gareth is very cheeky – not the little angel that everyone thinks he is, in a good way! He's just cheeky and there's no other word for it. When you meet him, you can't help but think he's a quiet person because of his stammer. It took a long time to get to know him because of that. I still think he was extremely brave to enter *Pop Idol*.

Thinking about them all now, I feel very privileged to have spent time with them – it was an incredible and very special group of people. We all had our moments of tears (especially when people were leaving), but I don't think any of us would have changed it for the world!

TUESDAY, 19 FEBRUARY 2002

Recorded the show today which was weird because I really preferred it when we did it live – there didn't seem to be the same energy today. I did have a great time with the audience though because the sound got mucked up for my duet with Gareth and I kept forgetting that my microphone was still switched on and they would hear me say, 'Oh bugger' or something, and then I realised that they'd heard! Honestly, I must have just looked like a bumbling fool – tried to blame the jet lag! Rachel from S Club 7 joined in for a duet with Gareth and it sounded great. Darius came on, Zoe was there, and I did my duet with Hayley – wonderful! Ant and Dec were hysterical – we had this thing where we would test our microphones to see if they were on before we spoke to each other and we'd blow into them first and then I'd say something to them and vice versa!

Anyway, finished recording the show and then there was a massive wrap party – they played a tape with all the songs we'd sung on the show and each of us in turn had to mime along to our own voices! It was the end of *Pop Idol* so although it was a brilliant night, I was really sad, too. What will I do on Saturdays from now on? Well the other nine contestants haven't got rid of me that's for sure, because in March we're going on a *Pop Idol* tour – I know we'll have a laugh!

WEDNESDAY, 20 FEBRUARY 2002

Very hungover but I went to my fave café for lunch and ended up on a café crawl around west London with all my friends. It was wonderful – I felt like my old self all over again until I got recognised! But as someone pointed out, I'm the Pop Idol and I'm going to get recognised!

THURSDAY, 21 FEBRUARY 2002

Up early for a promotional photo shoot in Fulham. Arrived about 9.30am and sat down for a chat with Jenny from 19 and Faye. Met the photographer, David Venni, who also came out with me to Cuba to take some promo shots – I think I forgot to write about that. Anyway, he's an excellent photographer so I was pleased he was behind the lens for today. Had so many text messages from friends today – apparently Robbie Williams had a jokey dig at me in his Brit Award acceptance speech last night and it's all over the papers today. Wow – I'm flattered! I can't believe Robbie would even know who the hell I was! Glad I didn't get to go to the Brits because let's face it I have done absolutely nothing – I've only been a full-time pop star for a week and a half! That seems very strange writing full-time pop star. After the photo shoot I had a meeting at the 19 Management offices in Battersea with Simon Fuller and Nicki Chapman. Everything they said I agreed with – I really do feel that we're on the same wavelength about my career. We talked press, my single, quality not quantity, doing things differently, not rushing the album – absolutely everything I wanted to hear. Brilliant – I think I'm going to be very happy. I trust them completely because we seem to have very similar ideas. Left the meeting then met Pilky for dinner and got wrecked.

FRIDAY, 22 FEBRUARY 2002

Met Fi, who's just come back from France, so it was great to catch up with her. Then I had a massive meeting with my lawyer. I really wanted to get on top of things and he explained everything I needed to know. Then I drove home to my parents' house exhausted by legal issues!

'The Long and Winding Road'… to success (hopefully!).'

'At the winners' show.'

'Chilling out...'

'Cuba is a beautiful place.'

'Shooting the 'Anything is Possible' video and arriving home.'

'The Evergreen video.'

'At Top of the Pops – fantastic!'

SATURDAY, 23 FEBRUARY 2002

Settled down to watch the *Pop Idol Winner's* show. Mary came down to my mum and dad's, Rupert and his girlfriend were there, too, plus Emma and Jack – such a beautiful little boy. I've really missed my nephew during this competition but he's more than making up for lost time – he's already been in bouncing on my bed trying to wake me up! Milsy was home, too, and she came over – it really was a full house. Watched the show and actually I didn't like it – maybe it was because it wasn't live? Dad kept talking through it – I had to keep telling him to shut up. I was really pleased with the duets but I thought it was a shame that Gareth and I looked like we were in love with each other during 'Long And Winding Road'! We were told to keep on looking at each other, but perhaps not like that! Oh well, it will keep people talking. We both had a good laugh about it. Luckily, I think my performance on 'Ain't No Sunshine' more than made up for that cheesy moment!

SUNDAY, 24 FEBRUARY 2002

Up early and drove back to London to go to church –
although I have found out recently that this church is leaving the area in search of pastures new. It was important for
me to go because becoming a Christian has really helped me
through the massive changes in my life recently. Met Tom,
Andy and Adam for Sunday lunch, which was a laugh, and
then I came back to the flat to tidy up. I may as well make
the most of my time here because I have a horrible feeling I
might not be around much in the future!

MONDAY, 25 FEBRUARY 2002

Crikey – can you believe my single was released today? (And no, I haven't been to look at it in the shops – although maybe I should!) But that doesn't mean the work stops! Had to meet my new stylist today, Charty Durrant (sounds very exotic). She had loads of great ideas and she was extremely nice too – I think we're really going to get on. Then it was off to Aquarium studios to record the 'Beyond The Sea' track because we're releasing a *Pop Idol* big-band album – how cool is that!

Came home and did some washing and packed for Dublin – no I'm not supporting S Club 7 again but I am going to do some song writing with two very cool producers!

TUESDAY, 26 FEBRUARY 2002

How cool is this? As I was boarding the plane to Dublin this morning Nicki Chapman phoned me to let me know that 'Evergreen' had sold 330,000 copies in one day! I did work experience at Sony Records a couple of years ago so I know how incredible it is. Nicki didn't think I seemed very excited but I had to explain where I was (i.e. on the plane) so I couldn't go loopy! I was so happy but I had to keep it under control.

Went straight to the studio and worked my arse off with Biff and Julian who are both very cool and have written some great pop tunes between them. Then Faye and I decided to hit the town. We're getting on much better these days and I'm really enjoying her company. Hit the Dublin bars and then ended up in U2's club The Kitchen and had a good old dance. It was great just to let go and have a laugh! Must admit had quite a lot to drink and am not feeling too good on it.

WEDNESDAY, 27 FEBRUARY 2002

Had a proper full day working in the studios – and with a hangover it's no fun but hey, gotta be a professional now! Wrote some great stuff today and am really pleased. Wonder if any of it will get used on my debut album? I'll just have to wait and see, I suppose! Found out today that I'm going be performing for the Queen! One minute I'm joking about having tea with Her Majesty and now I'm being invited to play at Buckingham Palace on 3 June alongside Sir Paul McCartney and Sir Elton John in a concert to celebrate the Queen's Golden Jubilee – save a sausage roll for me, ma'am!

Too much excitement for one day – having an early night!

THURSDAY, 28 FEBRUARY 2002

I'm still here and having the time of my life even though I'm working hard. Biff and Julian are great and the Irish people are all so wonderful – I really do like it out here. Checked out of the hotel and went straight to the studio, where we worked all day.

FRIDAY, 1 MARCH 2002

Got in late last night but had to be up early this morning for another meeting with Charty then it was off to the Aquarium again for more big-band recording. I cannot wait to hear this album – it's going to sound amazing! Then I had to record a phone interview for *CD:UK* tomorrow in the car on the way to making my ear mould for the *Pop Idol* tour! I know you wouldn't think it but getting this earpiece means that we're getting professional! Finished that and travelled to Home House where I was being interviewed by Simon and Miquita from the TV show *Popworld* – they were quite funny actually. Had a great laugh with them. I just try to get on with interviewers, rather than going in thinking I'm about to be grilled. I like to think of it as having a chat. Does that make sense or am I just rambling? Probably! Anyway finished that and then went to a fringe theatre production of *The Jungle* with Faye, Pilky and Milsy. There were only three actors – quite contemporary but very cool! Then we all went out for dinner and afterwards Milsy and I went back to

Pilky's house and danced till 4am to the Eurythmics, Boney M and the Jackson 5 – hilarious! Then Pilky and Milsy tried to convince me that they'd make great backing singers by trying to do harmonies for 'Evergreen' and 'Anything...' – definitely a case of don't call us we'll call you! Complete loonies, the two of them.

SATURDAY, 2 MARCH 2002

Met Charty again and got my outfits for *CD:UK* – she really has got my style down to a 'T'. Then went straight to the London Studios (same place as *This Morning*) to do a pre-record of both songs to be played on next week's show. Had to sing the two songs several times to make sure they had the one they needed – which is just as well because at one point Faye said you couldn't see me from the knees up on the monitors when they let off these pyrotechnics! I can see the headlines in the papers now: 'Will Decapitated From Knees Up' or 'Kneesy Does It!' So between that and the confetti that went everywhere… it went pretty well! Didn't get to meet the hosts though which was a real shame – hopefully there'll be another opportunity!

Oh my God – I find out if I'm Number One or not tomorrow. OK, so I have a pretty good idea that I AM Number One – but I'll find out just how many records I've sold because nobody is telling me! Keep your fingers crossed.

Got back to the flat and had a very strange evening –

strange because I didn't have anything *Pop Idol* going on. Had the urge to sit on the sofa – force of habit at 9pm every Saturday for the past three months!

SUNDAY, 3 MARCH 2002

Didn't have to be up early today, which was lovely! Went to church, came home and did a pre-recorded interview with Radio 1. Then Helen (lovely hair and make-up lady) came to the house to get me sorted before we had to leave to go to the Pepsi Chart HQ where I was going to be interviewed by Foxy while he ran down the last part of the charts! It was going to be transmitted around the UK! Was driven to Leicester Square and it had all been sectioned off... for me! There were loads of people – I think they must have thought Gareth was going to be there instead. I still find it weird that more people voted for me and I still think Gareth should have been the one to win just by the reaction he gets every-where he goes. Obviously I'm ecstatic I won but it's taking a long time to sink in! Eventually got into the building and met Foxy, four TV crews and some photographers – all squeezed into the studio!

So, the top ten singles were:

10. Beverley Knight – Shoulda Woulda Coulda
9.   S Club 7 – You
8.   R. Kelly – The World's Greatest
7.   Kylie Minogue – In Your Eyes
6.   Westlife – World Of Our Own
5.   Nickelback – How You Remind Me
4.   Lasgo – Something
3.   Enrique Iglesias – Hero
2.   Shakira – Whenever, Wherever
1.   Me – oh my God!!!!!

Foxy passed me an envelope to open on air – this contained just how many records I had sold. My hands were shaking as I ripped open the envelope and when I read the piece of paper I could have fallen on the floor. I had sold 1,108,659 singles. Unbelievable! Foxy told me it was the fastest selling debut single of all time – even beating Band Aid!

I was elated. Then he presents me with a plaque from the *Guinness Book Of Records* with my single on and it said 'Presented to Will Young to celebrate the Pepsi Chart Number 1 'Anything is Possible/Evergreen' and on becoming the fastest selling debut of all time.' Wow! Then Foxy tried to blind me with science by telling me that if you had taken all the songs in the Pepsi Chart from Number 2-200, added up all their sales and doubled it, I had still sold more than that! Bloody hell – it's gone mad!

Then to finish off the incredibleness of it all I had to introduce the very first play of Gareth's first ever single
'Unchained Melody' – scary or what!

Did a few interviews, had a few pics taken and then
came home. And do you know what I did? I unloaded the
dishwasher – how rock and roll am I?

Then went to Cally's house for dinner and just kept it all
quite chilled. In fact, it was probably one of the most relaxing but exciting days I've ever had!

MONDAY, 4 MARCH 2002

A special date has been added to the *Pop Idol* tour (which now stretches all the way into April) where all proceeds will go to the Prince's Trust, and today we went to meet some of the people who benefit from the money raised by them. It was so nice to see Gareth again – we haven't seen each other that much recently and have been communicating by text messages. Did our meet and greets, had a photo call and were presented with our very own Prince's Trust badges. After that I had some meetings at 19 to try and sort out my guest lists for the up and coming *Pop Idol* tour and I got to approve pictures of me to be used in the future. Then I left there with Nicki, Olivia and Faye for a meeting over at BMG, my record company, with one of the big bosses, Ged Doherty, Simon Cowell and many others. There was champagne, all the free CDs I could carry and I got taken on a tour of the building to meet everyone. What a laugh – I think I must have met most of the record company staff today. Had lots of pics taken, signed lots of autographs and was presented with another disc for my single going triple platinum – triple platinum! Bloody hell, is there anyone left to buy this song? Not that I'm complaining – it's just that the whole scale of this still amazes me! Tonight went out for dinner to celebrate Hayley's birthday along with Hayley (obviously!), Korben, Zoe and Gareth and some of Hayley's friends. Had a fantastic time – it was really nice to catch up and just have a normal night out.

WEDNESDAY, 6 MARCH 2002

Had a rare day off yesterday and had a major tidy up in
the flat. It was such a tip and I really needed to get it done.
If Mary came back and saw what I'd done to her home I
think she would have thrown me out! Got up early today
and I didn't mind one bit because I was doing an interview with Radio 4. Arrived at Broadcasting House and
went straight to the studio. It was so nice to meet the other
guests – Alan Titchmarsh, a singer/songwriter called
Peggy Segar and a new author called Pip Grainger. What
a lovely mixture of people. Have been hearing rumours
that there is a massive row kicking off with *Top of the Pops*
and BMG. Apparently *TOTP* won't let me perform both
sides of my song but BMG won't let me perform unless
both songs are played. No more Will versus Gareth, it's
now *TOTP* versus BMG! We'll have to wait and see what
happens. I've always wanted to perform on *TOTP!* Then it
was back to BMG to meet the people in charge of my internet site. Very exciting! Went through everything about

that with them, and it looks brilliant. Had the rest of the day off – hurray!

THURSDAY, 7 MARCH 2002

It's the start of our rehearsal for the *Pop Idol* tour – who'd have thought eight months after I filled an application form in that I would be on tour with nine of the most incredibly talented people around? We all met at the Marriott for vocal training with Ray Monk then were driven to John Henry's rehearsal studios for more vocal practise. On top of that we were taken to the LWT studios in Brixton so we could practise our routines with Kym Gavin, the live show producer! We had loads of dancers there and the floor was marked out exactly how the stage is going to be! This is going to be such a wicked show.

FRIDAY, 8 MARCH 2002

Exactly the same as yesterday – and we really did work our socks off because we all want these shows to be perfect. It was all going really well until I was told by the press office that there were these stories circulating around the press about me being gay – some bloke was trying to sell a story that he had slept with me. Bit difficult seeing as I'm celibate – oh and I don't even know him! Stories had already been touted around that I was gay at the beginning of the final ten but so far nothing's been printed. Today it's all kicked off. Basically, something that is no big deal to me has become a big deal. Deep breath... I am gay, all my family and friends have known that I am – so personally I don't see what all the fuss is about. In fact, Jessica asked me the first time she met me. She said in her wonderful Welsh accent, 'I hope you don't mind me asking, but are you gay? Don't mind me, I'm plain speaking.' That's exactly what Jess is like. 'Hello, you funny little Welsh girl, yes I am gay,' I replied. Then she said, 'I hope you don't mind me asking,

Will. Some people think I'm rude.' I didn't think she was rude at all and told her so. And that's how, in one way or another, the others found out. It's not a problem for me – in fact I think it's quite dull!

So this evening I had to meet with the press officer, Charlotte, to discuss things over a can or six of Stella. I decided I'd rather tell the public myself than have someone sell a salacious story about me which wasn't even true. We will release a statement to the press tomorrow. Luckily Rupert's come over and we just spent the evening talking about how crazy things can become. Come on fans, don't let me down! I think they're more discerning than that (please?!)

SATURDAY, 9 MARCH 2002

The press release went out to the papers this morning but got a phone call to say that the *Daily Mail* had already run an extremely nasty piece on me. This lady had never met me and yet for some reason felt the need to write a very negative piece based on... I'm not sure what! But I read it and by the end of the article I just felt sorry for her. I just thought, what kind of person can sit down and write an article like this with absolutely no knowledge of who I am and what I'm like? So as you can imagine I went to rehearsals in a really good mood – and then to top it all, I spoke to several of my friends who one by one told me that they had had journalists ringing them non-stop for the last two weeks! For God's sake – what is going on? Feel bad for all my friends but I know they will cope with it all. Worked hard again at rehearsals – well, I had enough stress to get rid of. Got home and decided to stay in and chill out by myself. Tomorrow is going to be an interesting day!

SUNDAY, 10 MARCH 2002

Well it's all over the papers today! I had a very weird moment when I went to buy some chewing gum at the newsagents and I looked at the counter where the *News of the World* had in large print WILL: I'M GAY! I looked at the bloke behind the counter, he looked at me and then I just smiled as if to say 'I'm afraid it's true!', paid for the chewing gum and walked out. I didn't read any of them – what's the point? Luckily, according to Charlotte, most of them were very supportive.

Spent the rest of the day really getting into writing with Cathy Dennis – it was very hard work because she's such a perfectionist. This evening I went over to Fi's house for a massive Sunday dinner with loads of friends from uni. I was pretty stressed for a while but after a while I relaxed and appreciated the company a whole lot more.

MONDAY, 11 MARCH 2002

Wrote all day with Cathy again and then got back and had to go shopping for a mini dinner party tonight. Had a bit of a panic attack as I walked into Tesco and suddenly thought everybody knew practically everything about me and I didn't like it. But you know what, I wasn't even recognised! Nobody cares about whether I'm gay or not by the sounds of the papers. Tried to cook fajitas for David, Carrie, Gareth, Jo, Claire and Rupert but it didn't go very well at all. Well, the cooking didn't but we still managed to have an excellent night anyway.

TUESDAY, 12 MARCH 2002

They've moved the rehearsals to a massive studio so that it replicates the arenas we're going to be performing in. It didn't go well for me and I kept mucking up my lines, which is not good for the moods! But I really do think that I'm one of those people who works better with a crowd. The shows are going to be out of this world – all ten of us are so excited because it's gone from a one-off show in London to a national tour consisting of 22 dates around the country. Mad! The first half of the show will have all of us performing by ourselves, coming on stage in the order that we left the *Pop Idol* show, so Korben is first on and so on. It ends with me singing 'Light My Fire' and 'Evergreen'. Then during the interval the stage will be set for the big-band songs – performed with the Big Blue. The audiences are in for a treat!

THURSDAY, 14 MARCH 2002

Went to Charty's house this morning – I've asked her to find me two outfits for this *TOTP* performance. At last I will get to perform both songs on the show. Cool! I think it got blown out of all proportion, although it's good to know that the team around me stand up for what they believe in.

Have been desperately trying to practise my moves and my links for the live shows to Faye, who has been doing hilarious impressions of an audience. It's our first *Pop Idol* show tonight at Wembley and I'm really looking forward to it. I get to finish both parts of the show, first and second half, and I have decided that maybe that's why I won – because it must be my natural place to be at the end.

POSTSCRIPT

So, that was it – my diary of an amazing few months. Perhaps what's more amazing is the fact that I managed to keep writing it! But I'm so glad I did because it'll be brilliant to read in a few years' time – and who knows where I'll be then? I've achieved my ultimate ambition – to have a career in music – but I know there's no guarantee that I'll still be around in ten years. Or maybe being a pop star won't be what I imagined and I won't be able to handle the pressure! But having got so far, I really do want to make it work. When I got to the final 100 in the *Pop Idol* auditions I'd already decided that I really wanted to be a singer – and it wasn't just some naïve little dream because I suddenly knew I could actually go out there and do it. I'm not sure I would have been able to go back to college even if I hadn't won – I was just too impatient! Having said that, though, I don't think I could have made it this far if it wasn't for the five weeks I spent at the Arts Ed because I needed to feel trained. I found it hard to go back to a school environment after university but it was really, really worth it. It made working with David, Carrie and Mike easier because I knew how to go through a score – and I even knew to have a bottle of water and a pencil with me every day! I felt really professional – much more so than when I went into the auditions. All my inhibitions went.

Overall, the whole *Pop Idol* experience was a positive one, not least because of all the fantastic people I met and the wonderful friends I've made. Hopefully everyone else in the final ten – Gareth, Darius, Zoe, Hayley, Rosie, Laura, Aaron, Jessica and Korben – will be successful, and I think it's safe to say we all benefited from the competition. Out of the ten I got on best with Hayley – we were the same age, we both smoked for England and we both liked a beer. She's very sweet and very easygoing and I know we'll always be friends. That's not to say that I didn't get on with the others, though – everyone was so supportive and there honestly wasn't any rivalry or nasty competitiveness. On the contrary – we'd all be in the dressing room together giving each other advice and support! Don't worry, I don't include the judges when I say I got on with everyone – although I suppose they had their jobs to do. What you saw on TV was very much what they were like once the cameras stopped rolling. They were extremely professional and kept their distance and you can't help but respect that. However, if there were a *Judge Idol* competition, I know who I'd be voting off… it would have to be Simon!

Pop Idol didn't just show the judges in a truthful light –
how you saw the contestants was how they really were.
They could have edited me in any way they liked and I
was really worried that they'd portray me as a posh boy
who failed in a boy-band competition. It could so easily
have been used against me and people who were in my
week could have had preconceived ideas about me. That's
why I was pleased I was hardly shown and what they did
show of me was all nice. I wanted to start the final 50 on an
equal footing, which I did, and it was like, Where has this
guy come from? Most people knew about Zoe (what a
voice for one so young), Gareth (who could hardly speak
but sang like an angel), Darius (well, everybody knew
Darius!), Jessica (she loved Pete Waterman!), Korben (he
looked and sounded the part) and Rosie (well, she was
famous for reducing Pete to tears!). Aaron, Laura, Hayley
and I were the ones who weren't shown much up to that
stage. But while I'm pleased with the way I was shown, the
filming aspect of the competition was extremely tiring.
The cameras followed us everywhere and I felt they
invaded our privacy at times. Poor Darius got the worst of
it though – having to be filmed shopping and cooking for
us all!

I loved every minute of the live shows – apart from the
sofas! They were the most uncomfortable things I've ever
had to sit on but I suppose it was good because it meant we
all had perfect posture – if you sat any other way you were

in pain! It was so hard trying not to wet myself laughing when I had to speak to Ant and Dec. They would always pick me in dress rehearsals to be the one that left – the bastards! I could never look them in the eye during the live shows, so believe it or not I always looked at Ant's ear! See, there are lots of secrets you didn't know about at home! The thing about Ant and Dec is that they're the same off TV as they are on TV – funny and down to earth. They were very professional and extremely good at their job – and they were always ready with a little quip or joke. Live presenting is such a difficult job – I hadn't appreciated that before.

So far fame isn't what I thought it would be – yes, there are plenty of perks, but it's opened my eyes on society. I've learnt a lot since winning the *Pop Idol* competition, and I've learnt a lot about myself, especially for something like this book. For one thing, I never thought my diary would cover 240 pages! thank you for sticking with me, reader! Without doubt, I think the most difficult part of being famous is the way it has touched everyone close in my life. My family and friends don't treat me any differently. There's a few who are quite insecure about me staying in touch – you know, those friends who we all have that are like, 'You never ring me,' but I really do have a valid excuse for not calling them maybe as often as I should. It's not intentional. I'm still the same Will I always have been – just a few more people know me now and I'm a little bit busier!

Looking back now, 'Ain't No Sunshine' was a massive

turning point for me – well, both for myself and for the competition. So many people have talked about it since but it's weird – where did that song come from? Why did I think about it when I was in the shower? It just popped into my head from nowhere – I hadn't heard it for ages. The more I think about it, the more I'm sure Karen Marsh had a hand in my fate, and I will be forever grateful to her for that. There are a lot of other people who have been there for me throughout all of this. I thank them all individually for their patience, support, advice and love... Annabel and Robin, Emma and Rupert Young, Meme and the rest of my wonderful family, my friends Cally and the Preston family, Adam, Andy D, Andy M, Scottish Tom, Squires, Abi, Milsy, The Frog, Hugh, Stavros, Janie (No.1 Fan) Hope, Katie, Mary, Sophie, Max, James (my oldest friend), Diana and Emily, the WHOLE *Pop Idol* team, Howler and Jo, Rachel and Ceilia, David and Carrie Grant, Ray Hedges, Mike Dixon, Tony, Toni and Nicole, all at 19, Faye, Simon, Nicki, Cathy Dennis, Oscar Paul, BMG, the Bryant Family, all at ITV2, Ant and Dec, Kate Thornton, everyone on the campaign bus, Fountain Studios, Charlotte Hickson and all at Henry's House, Gerrard Tyrrell, all at Arts Ed (especially Marianne), Exeter Footlights and everyone in Exeter. And special thanks to Bobby, my grandfather, who has been watching down on me the whole time.

But most of all I must thank you for voting for me – without you I certainly wouldn't be where I am today. It's still hard to believe I've had a Number-One single with 'Evergreen' and 'Anything Is Possible'. I'm not going to lie – I did find both the songs incredibly difficult to get my head round at first but I really do adore them now and they remind me of an incredibly exciting time in my life. Now I'm looking forward – the second single 'Light My Fire' is out in May and I'm performing for the Queen at her Golden Jubilee celebrations in June. I'm hoping to do some more live gigs and get on with a lot more song writing, work on the album (which is due out this year too) and then release a third single! Oh, and hopefully I might have made a bit of money in between – so I'm going to have a holiday and hopefully buy a house. Very important! And yes, I've still got the key to the chapel where I practised all those months ago – the curate must be going, 'Now where did I put my spare key?' I will return it, I promise!

The best thing of all, though, is that I'm determined to try to enjoy every moment this opportunity brings. They said anything is possible… they were damn right!